PARENTING

PARENTING

GETTING *IT* RIGHT

BIBLE STUDY GUIDE PLUS STREAMING VIDEO
SIX SESSIONS

ANDY & SANDRA
STANLEY

HarperChristian Resources

Parenting Bible Study Guide
© 2023 by Andy Stanley and Sandra Stanley

Requests for information should be addressed to:
HarperChristian Resources, *3900 Sparks Dr. SE, Grand Rapids, Michigan 49546*

ISBN 978-0-310-15841-7 (softcover)
ISBN 978-0-310-15842-4 (ebook)

HarperChristian Resources titles may be purchased in bulk for church, business, fundraising, or ministry use. For information, please email ResourceSpecialist@ChurchSource.com.

First Printing January 2023

Contents

Introduction

Parenting is a whirlwind.

It constantly requires you to figure out what's needed. And what's needed keeps changing!

With babies you learn how to feed, burp, change, bathe, clothe, and console. You learn how to help them sleep through the night and how to make them smile. You talk to other parents, read all the books, and take the classes, but experience is often the best teacher. And no matter how much you learn or how well you figure things out, a question lingers in the back of your mind: *Am I doing it right?*

As your children grow and develop, you figure out new skills to meet the needs of each age and stage. Just when you feel confident that you've mastered one task, something new and unexpected pops up. Even after your kids mature through adolescence and make that long-awaited entry into adulthood, you're still on the sidelines cheering them on and praying they've acquired what it takes to thrive on their own.

Regardless of how young or old your child may be, that initial, disquieting question always returns. Sometimes you're pretty sure you've got the parenting thing under control. Other times you feel like a failure.

Most of the time, though, you wonder, "Should I be doing more? Less? Something else entirely? Am I doing this right?"

When it comes to your kids, you don't want to wonder. You want certainty, confidence, and clarity about how to excel as the parent of the children gifted into your care. If there's one area of life you want to get right, it's parenting.

That's why you're beginning this video study on *Parenting*. As you'll discover, getting it right depends on how you define your "it"—the goal of your parenting. Often, in the midst of the crazy, it's hard to pause and think about what the end goal actually is. It's easy and far more intuitive just to drift in the direction of what we already know—how our parents parented. Or we simply focus on immediate behaviors and outcomes like safety, obedience, achievement, success, or the fulfillment of our own deferred dreams.

Whether you're aware of it or not, you are parenting in a direction. If you don't hit pause and consider the direction of your parenting, you may one day realize that you parented in the wrong direction—a direction you would not have chosen had you stopped long enough to choose.

In life and in parenting, direction determines destination. The direction you choose, consciously or unconsciously, will largely determine your children's destination. The direction you choose for your parenting has the potential to affect your kids emotionally, relationally, and spiritually, as well as academically and professionally.

You are parenting your children in a direction.

You owe it to them to choose it ahead of time—to lead deliberately rather than to react defensively or passively. Parenting is complicated. You want to get it right. To do that, you must determine your *it*. We hope this study guide plus the streaming video, as a companion to reading *Parenting*, will help you define your goals, find your bearings, and choose your *it*!

Andy and Sandra

How to Use This Guide

As you'll discover throughout this study, defining your goals for parenting and moving toward them require engaging with others as well as time alone for processing and applying what you're learning. As Andy and Sandra make clear in *Parenting* and in the video teachings of this study, they don't have all the answers or promise to make you a perfect parent. They do have practical experience raising three children and a bit of professional experience as pastors, teachers, and leaders. Learning from them and the others in your group can make you a better parent as you move toward a predetermined destination. This study is designed to facilitate your journey.

Each session in the *Parenting Video Study* begins with a mixer question followed by the video teaching before diving into some directed discussion with your group. Even though you'll find a number of questions provided to facilitate your group discussion, don't feel like you have to use them all. Your leader will focus on the ones that resonate with your group and guide you from there.

The final component of each group session is called "Process Your Parenting." This is where this study might diverge from other studies you've done. Your group will engage in some practical exercises designed to bring the teaching home to you. Hopefully, you'll find them fun and helpful.

After each session, there's a personal study with three more opportunities to engage with the content of *Parenting* during the week. The personal study includes a section to help you reflect on a passage from Scripture (called "Pause"), a section on exploring and applying ideas from *Parenting* (called "Pursue"), and an activity to help you put what you're learning into action (called "Practice"). You are invited to do at least one of these activities between sessions and to use this study guide to record what you learned.

Starting in Session 2, there will be time before the video teaching to check in and share the previous week's activity and process your experiences as a group. If you're unable to complete the between-sessions exercises or are new to the group, don't worry. Hearing what others have learned will be rewarding enough.

Finally, remember that this is an opportunity to explore new ways of considering what it means to be the best parent you can be. The videos, discussions, and exercises are all intended to equip your mind and empower your heart so you're inspired to try things on your own and adapt them for parenting your children. So let's get started!

Note: If you are a group leader, there are additional instructions and resources in the back of this guide to help you lead your members through the study. Because some of the activities require materials and setup, make sure you read this over ahead of time so you will be prepared.

SESSION 1

Your North Star

Your relationship with your children . . .
is determined by the law of the harvest, not
the last-minute urgency of the final exam.

—*Parenting*, p. 5

Welcome

Before satellites and GPS, before travel apps and Google Maps, navigation often relied on a celestial system. For centuries, sailors, navigators, and travelers used the stars to help guide their journeys—in particular, the North Star, or Polaris, to use its proper name. While Polaris isn't the brightest star on any given night, it's often easy to identify no matter where you are in the Northern Hemisphere. And it holds a unique, relatively fixed position, providing immediate orientation for the direction north.

The reliability and consistency of the North Star have made it a popular, long-standing metaphor as well. Whether a "north star" refers to goals, values, destinations, or moral principles, knowing your north star provides greater perspective and points you in the right direction. It reminds you of the longer journey and not merely your immediate location. Keeping your north star in sight prevents you from getting distracted by obstacles and problems that might take you off course. It allows you to set and maintain your direction over the long haul.

Having a north star for parenting serves the same purpose. Your north star is the "it" you want to get right to ensure that your children receive the love, attention, provision, and wisdom you have to offer. Too often you may overlook the need for a guiding goal because of the daily demands and draining challenges of parenting. But that's all the more reason to take time to look at the long view and establish a parenting north star, which is our starting point for this first lesson.

Start

If you or any of your group members are just getting to know one another, take a few minutes to introduce yourselves. Then, to get things started, discuss the following questions:

- Have you ever established a north star in parenting your children?
- If so, how has it helped you stay on course?

Watch Video (21:00 minutes)

Play the video segment for Session 1 (use the streaming video access provided with the study guide). As you watch, use the following video notes to record any thoughts or concepts that stand out to you.

- Parents often wonder, "Am I doing it right?"

- To get *it* right, you have to determine your *it*.

- Direction determines destination. The direction you choose, consciously or unconsciously, will largely determine your children's destination.

- If you don't define and choose your *it*, it will be chosen for you.

- Caught up in the whirlwind of parenting without a north star, you usually react rather than lead toward a predetermined destination.

- Our parenting goal was to raise kids who enjoy being with us and with each other even when they no longer have to be. We parented with the relationship in mind.

- Your relationship with your children is determined by the law of the harvest, not the urgency of daily demands.

- Rather than cultivating codependency, develop independence, an essential ingredient for mutually satisfying relationships.

- Parenting with the relationship in mind leads to better relationships.

- Your children do not have the same relationship with *you* that you have with *them*.

- We should always choose our words with our role in mind rather than our children's size, age, or reaction in mind.

- Never argue with your children—you are their parent, not their peer.

- The unavoidable tension between a parent and their children builds relational strength.

Group Discussion

As you consider what you just watched, use the following questions to discuss with your group members these ideas, their basis, and their applications in your life.

1. When it comes to parenting, how often have you wondered, "Am I doing it right?" How often do you second-guess your decisions as a parent?

2. How would you describe the direction of your parenting until now? How do you think your children might describe it?

3. Would you describe your parenting style as more reactive or more deliberate? Why?

4. How does parenting with the relationship in mind resonate with the direction you want to take your family?

5. What does it mean for your relationship with your children to be different from their relationship with you? What does this look like in your family?

6. Do you agree that conflict between you and your children can make your relationship stronger? Why or why not?

Process Your Parenting

In this first session, you've started the process of exploring what it means to reconsider the way you parent and to determine your north star. Regardless of the age and stage of your children, and setting aside the various emotions that may be swirling inside, consider where and how your family will end up if you continue parenting in your present direction.

To start processing the principles in this first session, silently ask God to help you clarify your goal for parenting so that you will see a harvest in the lives of you and your children. Then answer the questions below before reconvening with the group.

- What is the harvest you want to see in the lives of your children as they mature into adults?

- What seeds are you planting and cultivating in your children's lives to produce this harvest?

- In one sentence, what is your north star for parenting? Write it below.

Now go around the group and allow each person to share their north star statement. You don't have to share, but getting brief feedback from the group can be a great way to begin processing the changes you want to make in your parenting.

Pray

Conclude your session by sharing any requests you would like the group to lift up in prayer. Thank God for bringing you together for this study so that you can help and encourage one another as you pursue being wiser, more intentional parents. Ask him to give you clarity, wisdom, and discernment as you proceed with this group study. Trust that your heavenly Father will equip and empower you to follow his example of a loving parent.

Between-Sessions Personal Study

Reflect on everything you've covered in Session 1 by engaging in any or all of the between-sessions activities that follow. Keep in mind that this part of the study is not about doing homework or following a set of rules. These activities are simply designed to maximize the opportunity for this study to help you grow in your faith.

First, you will *Pause* and reflect on a passage from Scripture related to the main points of your last group session. Next, in *Pursue* you will spend some time in prayer, seeking God's wisdom and guidance about who you are and how you parent. Finally, in *Practice* you will consider how to apply what you've been learning in simple and practical ways.

For the first personal study, you will also find it helpful to have read the introduction and chapter 1 in the *Parenting* book by Andy and Sandra, if you haven't already. This between-sessions personal study can help you see what's been missing in the way you parent and how you can be deliberate moving forward.

Pause

At the end of your group session, you began considering how you've been parenting and how you want to parent moving forward. Your north star will likely be clarified and reinforced as you complete the rest of this study. Considering the basis for your parenting goal is often a good way to begin, and there's no better model than God our Father. With his example in mind, read the following passage and then spend a few minutes answering and reflecting on the questions that follow.

> Those who are led by the Spirit of God are the children of God. The Spirit you received does not make you slaves, so that you live in fear again; rather, the Spirit you received brought about your adoption to sonship. And by him we cry, "*Abba*, Father." The Spirit himself testifies with our spirit that we are God's children. (Romans 8:14–16)

- What impact does viewing God as your Father have on your parenting?

- How does this passage support making the relationships with your children the north star of your parenting?

- What one area of your parenting do you wish were more godlike? How are you presently struggling in this area?

- What one area of your parenting already reflects God's character? What impact has it had on your children?

Pursue

Considering how you parent can be emotionally charged. It may stir up memories of your own childhood and how you were parented. It can also call to mind past struggles or even decisions you now regret about how you've related to your children. To move forward and grow as a parent, being deliberate about your destination and the necessary change of direction requires acknowledging where you are.

Lingering over past mistakes or growing defensive about your choices doesn't usually help. Instead, thank God for the gift of the children he's placed in your life, and seek his power, love, and patience in parenting them. Acknowledge your mistakes and shortcomings as a parent, seek forgiveness, and receive the gift of God's grace. Let go of feeling like you've failed as a parent and start moving in a new direction. Read the following passage and then answer the following questions.

Which of you, if your son asks for bread, will give him a stone? Or if he asks for a fish, will give him a snake? If you, then, though you are evil, know how to give good gifts to your children, how much more will your Father in heaven give good gifts to those who ask him! (Matthew 7:9–11)

- What are some of the good gifts you give to your children? What motivates you to give these gifts?

- What gifts has God given you in order to help you parent the children entrusted to your care?

- Do any of the ways you were parented prevent you from giving good gifts and being the parent you want to be?

- What one aspect of your parenting do you wish you could immediately change? Why?

Practice

As Andy shares in *Parenting* and in the video teaching, he greatly admired the dynamic he observed in Sandra's family. Once he became a parent, Andy became more aware of the way her family members enjoyed one another and remained connected across a geographic distance. He wanted the same kind of bond in the family he and Sandra were starting, which prompted their commitment to making their relationships with their children their north star.

Similarly, you have likely met or observed other parents whose style of relating impressed you. Perhaps you noticed the absence of conflict or power struggles. Or maybe the genuine care and attention family members showed for one another. Whatever it is, you noticed and formed a favorable impression. Now it's time to take it one step further in pursuit of emulating these qualities in the way you parent.

After thinking about the parents you admire, choose one of them with whom you can get better acquainted. It could be someone from work, church, your neighborhood, school, or community. Before your next group session, contact this potential parenting mentor and arrange to meet for coffee or a meal. Simply tell this person you admire the way they parent and would like to chat about what they've learned. While you'll want to keep the tone relaxed and conversational, you may find the following questions helpful to jump-start your time together.

- What are the current ages and stages of their children? What parental challenges are they currently facing?

- How do they see themselves relating to their children once they're adults? What are they doing now to have that kind of future relationship?

- Looking back to when they first became parents, how has their parenting style changed? What was the catalyst for such change?

- What has informed and influenced the way they parent? What's been their north star or guiding goal?

For Next Session: Before your group's next session, read or review chapters 2 and 3 in *Parenting*. Pay special attention to what each chapter has to say about the four stages of parenting.

The Four Stages of Parenting

Parents have to consciously adjust their approach as kids seamlessly transition from one stage to the next. Too many parents never do. Or they fall behind and are forced to play catch-up.

—*Parenting*, p. 26

Welcome

When you're parenting in the moment, it's often tough to know what approach might be most effective. Should you focus on the fact that your child broke a rule, so they should be punished? Or do you use that instance as a teaching moment to train your kids and emphasize what they should be doing? Or you might wonder if you should just stand back while they face the natural consequences of the situation.

One way to choose your response is to consider the stage of development your child is in. From birth to about five years old, they need discipline. This is the time to teach your child that there are consequences—both good and bad—to their actions. Next, from five to around twelve, they need training, including the *why* behind your rules and expectations. Your job as a parent is to train while you explain.

The coaching years come next, from about twelve to eighteen, when your goal shifts from correction to connection. Your goal during this stage is simply to keep your kids coming to you for guidance and support. As your children move into adulthood, you enter the friendship years with them. This is when you begin to enjoy the rewards of all you've invested in their lives.

Perhaps these stages seem fairly intuitive, even basic. But kids move from one stage to the next without thought or effort, but their parents don't. If you don't evolve your parenting as your child develops, you undermine your influence with your child. The four stages of parenting provide a road map to help you navigate the challenges you'll face and the celebrations you'll enjoy in the years to come.

Start

Go around the group and check in with everyone as you each answer the following questions:

- What was your favorite game or activity when you were a child?
- Have you played it with your children?

After everyone has checked in, feel free to share what you learned from your between-sessions personal study or what you've been processing since the previous session.

Watch Video (21:30 minutes)

Play the video segment for Session 2 (use the streaming video access provided with the study guide). As you watch, use the following video notes to record any thoughts or concepts that stand out to you.

- Whether you're preparing for parenting or have already started, knowing the four stages of parenting can help you adjust your approach as your children develop.

- The four stages of parenting:
  1. The Discipline Years (0–5 years old)
  2. The Training Years (5–12 years old)

3. The Coaching Years (12–18 years old)
4. The Friendship Years (18+ years old)

- In the **discipline years**, you teach your child that their actions have consequences—both good and bad. You want them to obey so they'll be safe, strengthening their obedience muscles through multiple reps and appropriate consequences.

- You can't discipline for every single infraction, and you shouldn't. So decide what specifically you will discipline for—such as disobedience, disrespect, and dishonesty—and be consistent.

- Use the words you've chosen—such as *disrespect*—when correcting and disciplining them. Similarly, praise and celebrate when they get it right. What is rewarded is repeated.

- *Someone* will discipline your kids. It can be you, starting early and being consistent while the stakes are lower, or it can be other authority figures—teachers, coaches, law enforcement, judges—down the road when the stakes are higher.

- In the **training years**, you explain the why behind rules and expectations. You train while you explain. Your goal in this second stage is to help your kids gain the skills and values they need to succeed.

- The skills you want your kids to have in public, you must train them for in private. Two strategies that help with this are *practices* and *redos*. Practicing manners, social behavior, and situational choices can be made into fun games you can do over and over.

- The **coaching years** are probably the toughest transition for parents. You thoughtfully and carefully take steps backward from the training season of life and focus on connecting more than correcting.

- Like a good coach, you're mostly on the sidelines, encouraging players to run the plays and respond to situations according to the training that came before.

- Your goal during this third stage is simply to keep them coming to you for guidance and support. Three strategies for connecting in this stage include:
  - Cultivate constant conversations.
  - Don't bail; let 'em fail.
  - Get interested in what interests them.

- Cultivate conversational environments based on studying each child's personality and patterns. Learn to listen and not freak out no matter what they may disclose. Keep them confiding in and trusting you.

- The **friendship years** allow you to reap the harvest you've sowed into the lives of your kids in the previous three stages. This fourth stage is when you relate to one another as adults and hope to enjoy one another's company, even when you don't have to.

- Tailoring your parenting strategies and approaches to the four seasons of parenting allows you to reap big benefits when they're adults.

Group Discussion

As you consider what you just watched, use the following questions to discuss with your group members these ideas, their basis, and their application in your life.

1. What are your impressions of these four stages of parenting? Were you already familiar with them, or are you just now considering them?

2. Which of the four stages do you view as the most challenging? Why?

3. Which of the four stages do you feel best equipped to parent? How can you use your own strengths and weaknesses to your advantage, regardless of your children's stages?

4. Have you used any of the strategies mentioned for the training and coaching years? What was your experience like?

5. What other tools, strategies, or tips would you include for any of the first three stages?

6. Describe how you envision the friendship years with your children. Does anything need to change now in order to improve your relationship with them later?

Process Your Parenting

As you consider the four stages of parenting, it's a good opportunity to learn from your group members. Focus on your experiences both with your own parents when you were growing up as well as whatever stages you may have experienced so far as a parent. Use the questions below to consider the cumulative wisdom you can glean by pooling your observations and experiences.

- What are the current ages and stages of your children? How would you describe your parenting style in each stage?

- Do you plan to make any changes in parenting your children in their current stages? Why?

- Is your parenting style similar to how your parents raised you, or have you been deliberate in parenting your own children differently? Why?

- What advice, wisdom, and strategies have you learned from other parents that have proven helpful?

- Finally, what have you learned about parenting that you would pass along to parents just starting out? What do you know now that you wish you had known then?

Pray

Go around the group and share any prayer requests you have, particularly as they relate to your parenting, your kids, and your family. Thank God for gifting you with the children in your life and for equipping and empowering you to love them as best you can. Ask him to give you patience during each of the four stages and to show you how to love your kids as your heavenly Father loves you. Trust that he's using this study to help you grow stronger, wiser, and more deliberate in parenting your children.

Between-Sessions Personal Study

As with the personal study after the first session, the following questions and exercises provide opportunities for further exploration of the material from the last session and help you apply them to your life and parenting style. Remember, these aren't intended to be homework or another obligation in your busy schedule. Don't feel guilty or disappointed if you choose not to complete these right now or if your other responsibilities, such as engaging with your children and meeting their needs, don't permit you enough time.

If possible, though, use this study to stay connected to what you've been thinking and feeling since your last group session as well as to prepare you for your next meeting. If you haven't finished chapters 2 and 3 in *Parenting*, you'll find it helpful to do so before completing this personal study. The more you learn about the four stages of parenting, the better equipped you will be to handle the unique challenges of each one. Space is provided for your answers, or you can use the journal or notebook you started last time.

Pause

Seasons, stages, and cycles of time feature prominently throughout the Bible, both individually and historically. You might even identify the four stages of parenting in God's relationship with the children of Israel. After delivering them from captivity in Egypt, God gave commandments and guidelines to Moses to enforce with the sometimes-rebellious Israelites. God disciplined his people as necessary.

As the nation of Israel turned back to God, he began training them to live harmoniously with him and with others. As with parenting in the training years, God often revealed why and how certain guidelines protected, nurtured, and strengthened his people. Faced with the ongoing challenges of having a sacred relationship with imperfect humans, God sent his Son, Jesus, to live on earth among them. Jesus certainly coached his disciples and all who had ears to hear on how they could know God and enjoy relating to him as their Abba Father.

Finally, Jesus gave us the gift of the Holy Spirit to be our friend, comforter, and guide. Because of God's grace through the sacrificial death and resurrection of Christ, we can now have an intimate relationship with our Creator and be with him for eternity in heaven. Consequently, many people discover they have a new perspective on parenting because of their faith and their ongoing relationship with God. To remind you of the lavish love of the Father, read Jesus's parable below and answer the questions that follow.

> There was a man who had two sons. The younger one said to his father, "Father, give me my share of the estate." So he divided his property between them.
>
> Not long after that, the younger son got together all he had, set off for a distant country and there squandered his wealth in wild living. After he had spent everything, there was a severe famine in that whole country, and

he began to be in need. So he went and hired himself out to a citizen of that country, who sent him to his fields to feed pigs. He longed to fill his stomach with the pods that the pigs were eating, but no one gave him anything.

When he came to his senses, he said, "How many of my father's hired servants have food to spare, and here I am starving to death! I will set out and go back to my father and say to him: Father, I have sinned against heaven and against you. I am no longer worthy to be called your son; make me like one of your hired servants." So he got up and went to his father.

But while he was still a long way off, his father saw him and was filled with compassion for him; he ran to his son, threw his arms around him, and kissed him.

The son said to him, "Father, I have sinned against heaven and against you. I am no longer worthy to be called your son."

But the father said to his servants, "Quick! Bring the best robe and put it on him. Put a ring on his finger and sandals on his feet. Bring the fattened calf and kill it. Let's have a feast and celebrate. For this son of mine was dead and is alive again; he was lost and is found." So they began to celebrate (Luke 15:11–24).

- Why do you suppose the father agreed to his younger son's request and gave him his inheritance right away? Why was this father willing to let his son risk failing?

- After he had squandered his money but before returning home, how did the son come to view his father differently? How did failing allow the son to see his father more clearly?

- Does the father's response to the son's return surprise you? How would you as the parent have handled the situation?

- What does this parable reveal about parenting throughout the four stages? What's required of you regardless of the stage your children are in?

Pursue

Think back for a moment to when you first discovered you were going to become a parent. Recall all the various emotions and thoughts that likely swirled inside you. Perhaps you read books, talked to parents you knew, and searched online to learn all you could about this new role you were entering into for the rest of your life.

At the end of your last group session, you considered what you now know about being a parent that you didn't know back when you first started this journey. Often parents have accumulated more knowledge, insight, and wisdom than they realize, no matter the current age or stage of their children. Use the following questions and prompts to write a brief letter to yourself back before your first child was born, focusing on what you believe you most needed to hear at that time.

- What do you consider your biggest need as an expectant parent (information, assurance, instructions, something else)?

- What's one lesson or truth you've learned about being a parent that you wish you had known starting out? How did you learn this lesson?

- When I look back at who I was when I first became a parent, I see . . .

- How has your faith in God changed since you became a parent? What has parenting taught you about God?

Okay, now write your letter!

Practice

In *Parenting* and in the video teaching, Sandra and Andy share some of the tools and strategies that have worked well for them in each of the four stages. You may already be using some of these in your parenting, while others might be new. Your experience likely depends on the stage(s) of your child(ren).

As you consider all that you've learned and processed about the four stages of parenting, now it's time to apply and explore this wisdom with your own family. Begin by assessing your child's current stage based on their age as well as the developmental behavior you've observed. Think about the way you have been parenting and one shift or change you would like to make in how you relate to your child(ren).

Use the following questions and prompts to set a specific goal—for instance, playing a training game for twenty minutes—before your next group session. Other examples include finding an opportunity to praise and celebrate your child's obedience (in the discipline years) or doing an activity you know your preteen loves (in the coaching years), with the goal of just listening. Depending on the number of children you have and the various stages they're in, you will likely want to set different goals for each child and their respective stage.

Child's name:

Child's age and stage:

Strategies and tools for this stage that were mentioned in the book, video study, or group discussion:

An area needing attention right now:

One change I can make in my parenting to address this need:

Day or time when I plan to engage with my child and exercise this change:

For Next Session: Before your group's next session, read through or review chapter 7 in *Parenting*. Between now and your next session, pay special attention to the words you use when communicating with your children.

The Role of Words

In a healthy parent-child relationship,
the parent's words continue to carry extraordinary
weight throughout the relationship.

—*Parenting*, p. 133

Welcome

You've probably heard that actions speak louder than words. But within the context of your parent–child relationship, words are abnormally loud—sometimes even louder than your actions. While most words carry *some* weight, parent-to-child words carry extraordinary weight.

Words play such a dominant role in the parent–child relationship that what's *not* said often impacts children more than what *is* said. You may not get hung up on what your friends, neighbors, coworkers, or even your spouse doesn't say to you. But like many people, you may stop in your tracks when considering what your parents never said to you—especially "I love you" and "I'm proud of you."

It's important to realize that you can influence the trajectory of your children's lives through words *not spoken*. Similarly, in addition to not recognizing and not saying what your children need to hear, you may forget to factor in the *weight* of your words. There's no perfect and proper script to follow, but the words you use and how you use them contribute significantly to the influence you wield in your child's life.

The goal of carefully considering your words, your tone, and your timing is not merely to build and protect your kid's self-esteem. The reason is not so your kids will think you're the best, kindest, most eloquent mom or dad ever. The reason to get your words right, both spoken and unspoken, is because of the influence they can have. Basically, two things govern a child's respect for their parents: what they *say* and what they *do*. So what you say and how you say it probably matters more than you realize.

Start

Go around the group and check in with everyone as you answer the following questions:

- What three words best describe your parenting during the past week?
- Would your kids choose the same three words?

Finish checking in by discussing your experiences with the between-sessions exercises and activities. What have you learned from completing these personal studies?

Watch Video (22:30 minutes)

Play the video segment for Session 3 (use the streaming video access provided with the study guide). Use the following video notes while you watch in order to record any ideas or points that stand out to you.

- While most words carry *some* weight, parent-to-child words carry extraordinary weight. Words play such a dominant role in the parent-child relationship that what's *not* said often impacts children more than what *is* said.

- While the words and tones we choose have the power to build and protect our children's self-esteem, our words have the power to preserve something equally if not more important—*influence*. As parents, we want to preserve our influence as long as possible.

- Whether you realize and leverage them or not, three dynamics determine how your children process what they hear when you speak.

- First, **words are not equally weighted**. Negative words always weigh more than positive words.

- Next, **source determines weight**. Your words to your child carry extraordinary weight.

- When correcting your child, remember to communicate your approval of *who* they are along with your disapproval of *what* they've done.

- Source determines weight. Weight determines impact. Impact determines outcome.

- Finally, **intent is irrelevant**. There is no correlation between *intention* and *outcome*. Unintentional impact still leaves a mark that requires healing.

- Don't blame your kids for what they feel when your words hurt them. Their hurt is immediate and recovery takes time. Don't force proximity or coerce forgiveness from your children following your hurtful words.

- While these three dynamics are not at play in every conversation, all three remain in play in every season. Your words as a parent will always carry weight and have influence.

Group Discussion

As you consider what you just watched, use the following questions to discuss with your group members these ideas, their basis, and their application in your life.

1. Do you agree that parent-to-child words carry more weight than words generally carry? Why or why not?

2. How do the words you use, along with the way you use them, determine the extent of your influence in your child's life?

3. Why do negative words tend to weigh more than positive ones? Why do you suppose the impact of negative words often lingers longer than that of positive words?

4. Have you experienced your words landing heavier with your child than you intended? How does the source of words affect the weight they carry?

5. What was your immediate thought when you heard "intent is irrelevant"? Do you agree that if your words hurt or damaged your child, what you intended doesn't matter?

6. On average, how often do you apologize to your children for something you said? Can you describe a recent situation when this happened?

Process Your Parenting

Every time you speak to your children, three dynamics determine what your children hear and feel regardless of what you say:

1. Words are not equally weighted.
2. Source determines weight.
3. Intent is irrelevant.

With these three dynamics in mind, share with the group how you have experienced each of these dynamics in your own parenting. Don't use only negative examples that reflect how your words have wounded. And don't include only situations illustrating when your words were especially life-giving and encouraging. Instead, try to look back at recent situations or conversations with your child that reveal one, two, or all three of these dynamics in play. Use the following questions to reflect on and process the impact each dynamic has had when you have spoken to your child.

Words are not equally weighted.

- Have you ever noticed how your child reacted or responded to what you said to them? What stood out to you?

- Think about a time when you have spoken to your child to help counterbalance negative words they received from someone else—a sibling, classmate, friend, teacher, or coach. Did your words have the effect you desired? How could you tell?

Source determines weight.

- When have you been surprised by the weight your words carried with your children? When have you wished your words carried more weight than your child indicated?

- How effective is your sense of timing when speaking words to your kids? Do you sometimes say more than you should or miss opportunities and wish you had said more?

Intent is irrelevant.

- Do you agree with Andy and Sandra that sarcasm is dangerous and should not be used within your family? Why or why not?

- Do you tend to apologize quickly when your words hurt your child or to shift blame and make excuses? How does your tendency reflect your own experiences growing up?

Pray

Conclude your session by sharing any requests you would like the group to lift up in prayer. Thank God for the gift of language and the ability you have as a parent to positively influence your children. Ask him to grant you the right words at the right time. Offer thanks for the gifts of forgiveness and grace.

Between-Sessions Personal Study

As you've done before, use these questions and exercises to enhance your understanding of the material you've been learning from your reading and group sessions. Now that you're becoming more aware of the impact and influence you have in your children's lives, consider how your faith can help you be a better, more loving parent.

Let this personal study be a way to process any changes you wish to make in how you relate to your children. Trust that God will empower you and show you the way to strengthen your relationship, including your communication, with those he's entrusted to your care. Once again, jot down your answers in the space provided or continue using the journal or notebook you've started.

Pause

Words are the primary way most parents communicate with their children. But as with other aspects of parenting, you may not have given much thought to the words, phrases, tones, and attitudes you use regularly. Most parents have default ways they speak to their kids, which can have a cumulative impact, either positive or negative. Perhaps the starting point in using your words more deliberately and thoughtfully is simply to become more self-aware of the ways you communicate with your children, both spoken and unspoken.

Toward that goal, spend a few minutes assessing the language you often rely on when speaking to your children. The old adage encourages us to "think before we speak," and you may have even said as much to your kids, but slowing down to practice this isn't always easy. Thinking back on the words you've used and the ways you've communicated with your children during the past week, look for aspects you want to change or improve. Use the questions below to facilitate your assessment.

- How would you describe your current communication style with your kids? Does it reflect their current stage of development?

- What words and phrases do you use most often to convey correction or disapproval? How effective do they tend to be?

- Similarly, which catchphrases and words do you use when expressing approval and encouragement to your children? How effective do you believe they are?

- What word or sentence did you use recently that you wish you could take back? Why?

- When you realize that your words have been hurtful to your kids, what do you usually say or do next?

- How would you describe the way you want to communicate with your children in this season of their lives? What do you need to say more often to them?

Pursue

Throughout its pages, the Bible emphasizes the power of our words. Simply put, God cares what we say, how we say it, and the effect our words have on others. Many of the wisdom verses in Proverbs focus on the impact words have, both to give life and to wound grievously: "The soothing tongue is a tree of life, but a perverse tongue crushes the spirit" (Proverbs 15:4).

When words and the power of the tongue are mentioned in the New Testament, it often emphasizes the correlation between the words we speak and what's in our hearts. Jesus told his followers, "A good man brings good things out of the good stored up in his heart, and an evil man brings evil things out of the evil stored up in his heart. For the mouth speaks what the heart is full of" (Luke 6:45). One of the lengthiest passages addressing the power of our words occurs in James. Read through it below and then answer the questions that follow.

When we put bits into the mouths of horses to make them obey us, we can turn the whole animal. Or take ships as an example. Although they are so large and are driven by strong winds, they are steered by a very small rudder wherever the pilot wants to go. Likewise, the tongue is a small part of the body, but it makes great boasts. Consider what a great forest is set on fire by a small spark. The tongue also is a fire, a world of evil among the parts of the body. It corrupts the whole body, sets the whole course of one's life on fire, and is itself set on fire by hell.

All kinds of animals, birds, reptiles and sea creatures are being tamed and have been tamed by mankind, but no human being can tame the tongue. It is a restless evil, full of deadly poison.

With the tongue we praise our Lord and Father, and with it we curse human beings, who have been made in God's likeness. Out of the same mouth come praise and cursing. My brothers and sisters, this should not be. Can both fresh water and salt water flow from the same spring? My brothers and sisters, can a fig tree bear olives, or a grapevine bear figs? Neither can a salt spring produce fresh water. (James 3:3–12)

- Go back through the passage and underline all the comparisons James makes about the human tongue. Which one stands out to you or surprises you?

- Were there negative words spoken when you were growing up that still linger with you? Why did these words have such power to wound you?

- When have you spoken rashly and wounded someone you love? How did this incident affect your relationship?

- In addition to paying heed to the words you use, especially with your children, what do you want to teach your kids about the power their words can have? How are you teaching them this?

Practice

In chapter 7 of *Parenting*, as well as the last video teaching, Andy and Sandra emphasize the powerful impact that *unspoken* words often have. With most of our family, friends, and social acquaintances, we learn to "read between the lines" regarding what goes unspoken. Based on their body language, inflection, volume, tone, and expression, they can communicate a great deal to us with only a few words. We learn to make certain assumptions and inferences based on their personality, the relational context, and the social situation.

The power of parental words is different, though. There are words that every human being longs to hear from their parents—basically "I love you" and "I'm proud of you." While these may seem like messages every parent communicates to their children, not just once but frequently, many people never hear these words they long to hear. They may sense their mother's or father's love and implicitly believe that their parents are indeed proud of them. But there's a power in hearing those words and receiving them that cannot be overstated. You may, in fact, have similar words that went unspoken that you longed to hear from a parent.

Most parents want to use their words carefully and deliberately, conveying love and acceptance even when correcting, challenging, or expressing difficult emotions. Intending and doing are not the same, though. In the moment, in the pressures and problems of everyday life, many parents miss opportunities to provide the life-giving words their kids long to hear.

While your spoken words carry extraordinary weight, your written words are also incredibly impactful, depending on the timing, age, and stage of your children. It's not uncommon for parents to write a loving message when a birthday, Christmas, or another special occasion rolls around. But sometimes words reverberate the most during the course of an ordinary day.

Before your next group meeting, write a note of love and encouragement to your child for no reason other than to surprise and delight them. Make it age appropriate, of course: it can be a sticky note on the cereal box, a message in their lunch bag, a handmade card you mail to them, or a letter left in their room. Try to avoid ways you typically communicate, such as text and email. Try to make it something that will particularly appeal to your child and express your love, both in words and in action.

For Next Session: Before your group's next session, read or review chapter 9 in *Parenting*. Think about your own views on the relationship between marriage and parenting and the ways each one can affect the other.

SESSION 4

Marriage Matters

When it comes to parenting,
your marriage matters. It matters a lot.

—*Parenting*, p. 149

Welcome

Your marriage—your relationship with your spouse—and the attitude you convey about marriage all become part of the story your kids will tell, because we all have origin stories. If you think about it, anytime you get to know someone beyond a surface level, sharing your relationship status is part of the exchange. And for good reason.

Understanding someone's story and their attitude toward relationships and marriage often reveals a great deal about who they are and why they are the way they are. You've likely met people who stunned you with the situations and life events they've endured. Or you want to pepper them with questions about their family of origin and how their parents raised them to be so resilient and emotionally healthy.

Similarly, you have your own story and perspective on marriage. And the way your kids experience your views on marriage will be a significant part of their stories.

Your marital status and your views on marriage influence how your children move through the world, not just when they're teens or start dating, not just when they're young adults, but *now*. The emotional climate in your home affects your children's current and future well-being—all the more reason to prioritize and invest in your marriage or your most important human relationship.

Start

Check in with everyone in your group and complete the following:

Marriage is to parenting as _____ is to _____.

Feel free to share anything you discovered from your between-sessions personal study, such as aspects of your parenting you're changing or any ideas you've had since your last group meeting.

Watch Video (22:00 minutes)

Play the video segment for Session 4 (use the streaming video access provided with the study guide). As you watch, use the following video notes to record any thoughts or concepts that stand out to you.

- Whether we like it or not, our marriages are a big part of the parenting equation. Parents who get it right with their kids often get it right in their marriage relationships too. Strong marriages create a firm foundation for raising relationally healthy kids.

- Your relationship with your spouse becomes part of the story your kids will tell. Your marriage also influences how your children move through the world now. The emotional climate in your home affects your children's current and future well-being.

- You and your spouse are already a family before you have any children. To grow stronger in your marriage, consider these five practices for loving each other.

1. **Prioritize and invest:** Be intentional about making your spouse feel like the primary priority and invest in unique ways you can make your spouse feel like your priority.

2. **Be a student of your spouse** and act on what you learn. Know their love language and engage with what they care about.

3. **Be your spouse's loudest cheerleader.** It isn't your job to keep your spouse humble.

4. **Practice showing gratitude** because unexpressed gratitude communicates ingratitude.

5. **Harness the "aah factor,"** the sense of happiness and love that honors, strengthens, and communicates the powerful notion of "I'd choose you all over again."

- A healthy marriage is a relationship where mutual respect and mutual submission are the identified goals—even amid life's conflicts, struggles, or grief.

Group Discussion

As you consider what you just watched, use the following questions to discuss with your group members these ideas, their basis, and their application in your life.

1. What impact did your parents' relationship have on your view of marriage? How do you want your relationship with your spouse to shape the story your kids will tell someday?

2. What are some ways you prioritize and invest in your spouse? What has your spouse done lately to show that you are still their priority?

3. What have you learned about your spouse by studying them and discovering their love language? How do you typically communicate your love based on what you know?

4. Do you consider your spouse your loudest cheerleader? When have you experienced their praise and encouragement in a way that made you feel seen and loved?

5. What are your favorite ways to show gratitude to your spouse? How does your spouse communicate gratitude to you?

6. How would you define or explain the "aah factor"? Have you experienced it with your spouse recently?

Process Your Parenting

Like parenting, marriage is seemingly an inexhaustible topic when it comes to advice, how-to books, and counsel from both amateur and professional experts. Andy and Sandra offer their insights in the book and the video teaching along with five recommendations for strengthening and sustaining a healthy marriage.

Once again, your group members can also contribute their insights and practices learned in their own marriage relationships in order to establish and maintain a firm foundation for parenting their children. With this goal in mind, get in groups of three or four to answer the following questions as you discuss what has helped you improve your marriage and thereby benefitted your kids.

- What effects has having children had on your marriage? How do you and your spouse maintain a strong connection and prioritize each other when it's so easy to focus on your kids first?

- What habits and practices, other than the ones already shared in the teaching, have helped your marriage become healthier and stronger? What tips would you give newlyweds?

- How do you and your spouse handle conflict in front of your children? What do you want to teach your kids about how to handle hard things in a marriage relationship?

- How do you maintain a healthy boundary between your relationship with your spouse and your relationship with your kids?

Pray

As you end your time together with prayer, go around the group and share one request regarding your marriage or relational status. You don't have to go into detail or explain your request, but let others know enough so they can lift up your concerns. Then begin your time in prayer by thanking God for how you're learning and growing. Praise him for the many ways he is at work in your lives, equipping and empowering you in all your relationships. Ask him to continue to inspire you with his love as you seek to love those you care most about.

Between-Sessions Personal Study

You know by now that these questions and exercises are intended to help you explore more deeply the material you've been covering. As you grow in your awareness of how to be a better, more intentional parent, consider where you are in the process. Don't be discouraged if you feel like you haven't been parenting the way you want to. Simply ask God to meet you where you are and to give you strength and grace as you begin a new season in your relationship with your children.

Continue to record your answers and responses, either here or in your journal or notebook. If you haven't finished reading through chapter 9 of *Parenting*, now is a good time to catch up before your group's next session.

Pause

Depending on your relational status or the condition of your marriage, this topic can certainly stir up a volatile mix of thoughts and emotions. As Andy and Sandra acknowledge, their content is based on their personal experiences in two-parent families as well as their observations as youth leaders and foster parents. While your last group session focused primarily on how to strengthen and improve a marriage relationship, its aim was not to exclude single parents, divorced parents, or unmarried parents.

The main point is this: your attitude and actions about marriage, along with the relationship you may have with your coparent, directly impact your children's stability, security, and well-being. So even if you're not presently married or you consider your marriage to be strained or broken, how you regard a committed relationship matters. If you are married, then your relationship with your spouse provides a firm foundation for raising relationally healthy kids.

So now is a good time to pause and do a brief assessment that identifies and acknowledges your views on marriage as well as the factors contributing to your perspective. You may not realize or like what you have been communicating to your children about marriage, because, as you know, kids intuitively pick up on the emotional environment around them. Use the questions below to help you see more clearly what you believe about the correlation between marriage and parenting.

- Reflect for a moment on your last group session and the discussion you had. What is your biggest takeaway? Why do you suppose this point stands out to you?

- Regarding the topic of marriage, what concerned, troubled, or frustrated you in your group's last session? What did you most enjoy?

- What messages about marriage did you receive from your parents when you were growing up? Do you want to pass along the same messages to your kids? Why or why not?

- What comparison or metaphor would you use to describe the connection between marriage and parenting?

Pursue

Both in their book *Parenting* and in the previous session's teaching, Andy and Sandra describe a healthy marriage as a relationship where mutual respect and mutual submission to each other are the identified goals—even amid life's conflicts, struggles, or grief. This view of marriage is biblical and timeless, although many scriptural passages referencing marriage have historically and culturally been misunderstood, misinterpreted, and misused at times.

Because your beliefs about marriage directly affect your parenting, read through the passage below and reconsider what you've often assumed the Bible says about the relationship between a husband and a wife. Then answer the questions that follow.

Submit to one another out of reverence for Christ.

Wives, submit yourselves to your own husbands as you do to the Lord. For the husband is the head of the wife as Christ is the head of the church, his body, of which he is the Savior. Now as the church submits to Christ, so also wives should submit to their husbands in everything.

Husbands, love your wives, just as Christ loved the church and gave himself up for her to make her holy, cleansing her by the washing with water through the word, and to present her to himself as a radiant church, without stain or wrinkle or any other blemish, but holy and blameless. In this same way, husbands ought to love their wives as their own bodies. He who loves his wife loves himself. After all, no one ever hated their own body, but they feed and care for their body, just as Christ does the church—for we are members of his body. "For this reason a man will leave his father and mother and be united to his wife, and the two will become one flesh." This is a profound mystery—but I am talking about Christ and the church. However, each one of you also must love his wife as he loves himself, and the wife must respect her husband. (Ephesians 5:21–33)

- Considering this passage, why is faith important for a healthy marriage? How has your faith affected the way you view marriage?

- Why is mutual submission essential to a healthy marriage? Being as specific and concrete as possible, what does mutual submission look like based on your experience?

- What word, phrase, or instruction in this passage resonates with you? Why do you suppose it stands out?

- Have your views on what makes a marriage successful changed over the years? Why or why not?

Practice

Using all you've been reading, discussing, pondering, and processing about marriage, think about what you want your children to know about it. Marriage is certainly a complex topic requiring a certain level of maturity to understand and appreciate. Nonetheless, you have already been communicating some message about marriage to your kids, regardless of their ages and stages. So, as you've been doing with various aspects of your parenting, perhaps it's time to be intentional and more direct about the marriage message you want to send your kids.

With this goal in mind, use the following questions and prompts to help you express your message about marriage to your kids in ways that are concise, accessible, and age appropriate.

- What do you assume your children already believe about marriage? What factors have influenced the way your kids view marriage in general?

- Have you had direct talks with your kids about marriage? What do you suppose they took away from these discussions?

- Have you had direct talks with your kids about divorce, whether because of your own divorce or that of other family members, neighbors, friends, or classmates? How does your kids' awareness of divorce affect the way they view marriage?

Complete the following: **What I want my kids to know about marriage right now is . . .**

because

Before your next group meeting, plan to talk to your children (either individually or as a group, if appropriate) and share the marriage message you've expressed above. You can tell them that they're helping you with your homework or something similar in order to help them not feel pressured or put on the spot. If you believe it would be helpful, you can also show them a scene from a TV show or movie that illustrates the message you want them to take away from your talk. If possible, have this discussion with your spouse or coparent participating, although this is not essential. The focus should be on the intentional message about marriage you want your children to know at this time.

For Next Session: Before your group's next session, read or review chapters 4 and 5 in *Parenting*. Think about the ways you were disciplined while growing up and how this has shaped the way you discipline your kids.

Establishing Rules and Consequences

The goal of discipline is to teach your child how
to restore the relationship they damaged.

—*Parenting*, p. 78

Welcome

"No!"

"You know better . . ."

"How many times have I told you . . . ?"

Sound familiar? When your child misbehaves, what's your typical reaction? When they break a rule or act out or mouth off, what is generally the first thing you say? And what's their usual response?

The problem with your natural, go-to responses—or reactions—is that they put you and your child on opposing teams. Even if the transgression wasn't aimed at you, a typical reaction sets you up as the offended party. It may appear as if, and feel to your child as if, your relationship with your child is in jeopardy. You've become their adversary.

A better posture to take when your kid misbehaves is, *Oh no!*

Oh no! is siding with your child against their disobedience. Basically, your attitude and message express, *Oh no! We—you and I—are so sorry you did that because now you'll have to face the consequences. Oh no! I am for you, and I hate that you are going to be penalized for your behavior.*

An *Oh no!* reaction keeps you and your child on the same team relationally. They aren't off the hook, but you aren't the bad cop or mean judge. In addition, *Oh no!* has a practical benefit too. It buys you time. The length of time should be age appropriate, but *Oh no!* gives you time to calm down and think creatively. If you end up punishing your kids the same way every time regardless of the offense, you dilute your discipline. Creativity and context, however, allow you to tailor the consequences to fit the crime.

Start

Check in with everyone in your group and share your answer to the following questions:

- What do you usually say when your child misbehaves?
- What's your default, go-to punishment right now?

Finish checking in by discussing your experiences with the between-sessions exercises and activities. What have you learned from completing these personal studies?

Watch Video (20:00 minutes)

Play the video segment for this fifth session (use the streaming video access provided with the study guide). As you watch, use the following video notes to record any thoughts or concepts that stand out to you.

- Once we identified our *it* and committed to parenting with the relationship in mind, we realized that goal would need to inform both the rules we set and how we responded when our children broke the rules.

- Using our goal and approach, we established two overarching rules, both directly connected to establishing and maintaining healthy relationships: (1) Honor your mother. (2) Don't tell a lie.

- Honor is a decision and becomes a *keystone habit*, a single behavior that has ripple effects. Since Andy made the rule about honoring Sandra, he had to set the example and model it for their kids.

- Honoring Mom required prioritizing what's important to Mom, such as a clean room, a made bed, a respectful tone. This one rule saved us from having to make a bunch of other rules because it provided a relational *why* behind the *what*.

- We taught our kids that their irresponsibility eventually becomes someone else's responsibility.

- Honor your children's mother with your words, tone, and behavior and your kids will follow your example.

- When parenting with the relationship in mind, rules and discipline must be anchored to the preservation of relationships. This explains our second rule—"Don't tell a lie!"—because lying breaks relationships.

- Children must be taught, not simply expected, to tell the truth. Telling the truth requires coaching, and the earlier you begin the better.

- When confronting your children over something you know they may be tempted to lie about, make sure you're in a good place emotionally. This helps them avoid lying as a defensive, self-protective reflex.

- Ask yourself why you discipline your children—what's your goal or desired result? Focus on discipline, which provides direction and training rather than punishment, which is merely payback or a temporary deterrent.

- If you choose to parent with the relationship in mind, the goal of discipline is a restored relationship, not simply behavior modification. But restoring a relationship is a skill that must be taught.

- Discipline with the relationship in mind, and set rules that reflect how much you value the relationship. This approach may require more creativity, time, and involvement, but it produces results in your children that last a lifetime.

Group Discussion

As you consider what you just watched, use the following questions to discuss with your group members these ideas, their basis, and their application in your life.

- What has been the basis for the rules and discipline you have used with your children? How has this worked for you and for them?

- Do you agree that the rule "Honor your mother" has a greater impact than "Honor your parents"? Why or why not?

- Other than honor, can you think of other keystone habits you want to teach your child? How do these habits reflect your end goal?

- Do you believe children must be taught, not simply expected, to tell the truth? What experiences contribute to your answer?

- How would you describe the distinction between discipline and punishment? Do you agree that discipline is more effective? Why?

- What are some examples of creative consequences you have used when your children have misbehaved or broken the rules? How did these consequences reinforce your goal for parenting?

Process Your Parenting

Rules and discipline often reflect the personalities of the parents who create them. Some parents have many explicit rules, while others may have only a few that are more implicit. Some parents leap by default into a power struggle with their kids, while others may be more laid-back or even lax in enforcing rules and discipline. Intentionally or not, some moms and dads take approaches that fall into the good cop/bad cop routine so that one parent ends up being the angry enforcer, while the other is the compassionate comforter.

Regardless of your personality, consistency in your approach to rules and discipline is an essential element for achieving the results you desire, which is why it is so important to know *why* you discipline your kids. Nearly all parents want to invest in their kids' lives rather than getting them merely to conform to rules to avoid conflict. As a parent, you want to influence your child's character and instruct them so they can mature into a self-sufficient, emotionally healthy adult.

After identifying your north star for parenting, allow it to guide your approach to discipline and the rules you set. Rules and discipline provide trail markers on the path to the kind of adults your children will become and how you relate to them then. So spend a few moments writing down your parenting goal (which you started back in Session 1) and then expressing how you want your rules and disciplinary approach to reinforce this goal. Use the prompts below to get started.

The north star goal for my parenting is:

With this goal in mind, I want my consistent approach to discipline to be:

Based on my goal, along with my disciplinary approach, the rules that make the most sense for disciplining my kids now are:

Now look over what you've written and spend a few minutes sharing your approach and rules with the rest of your group. Feel free to revise them based on your discussion.

Pray

Go around the room and share any prayer requests, and then pray for those requests together, either silently or out loud or both. Ask God to give you wisdom and discernment as you seek to discipline your children the way he disciplines us—motivated by love. Thank him for the grace and mercy he gives you and the example this sets for how you correct, direct, and train your kids. Trust that he will inspire you with loving, creative, effective responses and consequences when faced with disciplining your children.

Between-Sessions Personal Study

As you consider any lingering thoughts from your last group session, use these questions and exercises to enhance your understanding of how to parent more intentionally, particularly regarding rules and discipline. Continue to record your reflections and observations, either here or elsewhere, so you can share them with your group if you want to at the beginning of the next session. Before you begin this week's study, make sure you have finished reading chapter 10 in *Parenting*.

Pause

Now that you're more aware of various approaches to discipline and setting rules, consider any possible changes you want to make in your relationship with your kids. Think about what you've been doing and how effective your previous tactics have been in achieving the results you want. Don't be afraid to tell your kids that you've decided to make some changes, explaining some of your rationale as appropriate. More importantly, be consistent in how you show them these changes.

Use the questions and prompts below to help you reflect on the way you've been disciplining your children and the way you want to discipline them moving forward.

My approach to parental discipline and rules up until now can best be described as:

What I see now about the way I've been disciplining my kids that I haven't seen before is:

- In light of what you've been reading and thinking about and discussing with your group, are there any shifts you want to make in how you correct and discipline your children? Why?

- Look back at the approach and rules you wrote down at the end of last session. Any changes, edits, or revisions you want to make to clarify or correct them? Write the revised versions of your rules below.

Pursue

It may seem obvious, but it's good to remember that disciplining your children should always be motivated by love. As you may have heard your parents say or even said yourself, "If I didn't love you, I wouldn't correct you." Responsible, loving parents know that a crucial part of their job is to instruct, influence, and equip their children for the demands of life. When you discipline them, you provide an opportunity for them to strengthen their character. Your discipline and corresponding rules reflect your love in action.

This is the kind of discipline we find described in the Bible, the kind God uses to instruct and fortify us as his children. With this parallel in mind, read the following passage and then answer the questions that follow.

Have you completely forgotten this word of encouragement that addresses you as a father addresses his son? It says,

"My son, do not make light of the Lord's discipline,
and do not lose heart when he rebukes you,
because the Lord disciplines the one he loves,
and he chastens everyone he accepts as his son."

Endure hardship as discipline; God is treating you as his children. For what children are not disciplined by their father? If you are not disciplined—and everyone undergoes discipline—then you are not legitimate, not true sons and daughters at all. Moreover, we have all had human fathers who disciplined us and we respected them for it. How much more should we submit to the Father of spirits and live! They disciplined us for a little while as they thought best; but God disciplines us for our good, in order that we may share in his holiness. No discipline seems pleasant at the time, but painful. Later on, however, it produces a harvest of righteousness and peace for those who have been trained by it. (Hebrews 12:5–11)

- Have you experienced being disciplined by God? If so, what impact, good or bad, did this divine discipline have on your relationship with God?

- Why must you not "lose heart when he rebukes you"? Is this the same reason you hope your own children do not lose heart when you discipline them?

- Considering this passage, what is the desired result when God disciplines his children? How does this parallel the desired result you want to achieve in your children?

- Do you agree that "no discipline seems pleasant at the time, but painful"? What is the eventual spiritual result of this suffering?

Practice

If you're fortunate, you won't have an immediate opportunity to put into practice what you're learning about rules and discipline. Most parents, however, don't know when their child might act out, show disrespect, or break a rule. It might be this evening or next week or beyond. All the more reason to practice the *Oh no!* approach and to have thought about creative consequences *before* you need to implement them.

Throughout *Parenting*, particularly chapters 4 and 5, Andy and Sandra share examples of creative, effective consequences for when their kids broke rules or damaged relationships. Now it's your turn to plan how you can take a similar approach. Use the questions and prompts below to brainstorm age- or stage-appropriate consequences for upcoming behavior violations in your home.

- What's your favorite story shared by Andy and Sandra? What do you like about it?

- Rather than taking away possessions and privileges, how can you discipline your kids to make a bigger point than simply that they disobeyed?

- Using your knowledge and understanding of your children, what are some unexpected consequences that might make lasting impressions?

Fill in the blanks: The next time my child does _____, I believe a creative consequence to reinforce the importance of my parenting goal would be _____.

For Next Session: Before your group's final session, finish reading all chapters in *Parenting.*

Think about the messages you received about God, faith, and religion as you were growing up.

Developing a Faith of Their Own

Don't let *your faith* get in the way of *your relationships* with your children.

—*Parenting*, p. 189

Welcome

Nearly every parent wants to leave a legacy to their children beyond monetary gain. If you are a person of faith, any faith, you no doubt hope to pass along your faith to your kids. In this pursuit, the good news is that your faith inevitably comes through in the ways you parent. Unfortunately, the bad news is also that your faith inevitably comes through in the ways you parent.

Once again, it's beneficial to be intentional about which aspects of your faith you want to give your children and how you want to pass these spiritual aspects along to them. And as you know, faith is deeply personal. It's something an individual chooses to embrace. So your *win* or the *it* as it relates to faith, is often simply helping each of your children develop a faith of their own.

Another important reason to be deliberate in knowing what you want your spiritual legacy to be is so you can be mindful of it in the daily trenches of parenting. When you consider the faith of your children, what's the win? What are you hoping and praying for? These are important questions because your *win* will determine your *role* in the development of your children's faith.

Plenty of people can teach your children the books of the Bible and the stories contained there. Only you can demonstrate day by day, season by season what it looks like to allow the teachings of Jesus to shape decisions and relationships. Nobody has a better opportunity than you to model for your children the sustaining power of faith in God during difficult times.

If you hope to provide your children with an enduring, robust, real-world faith of their own that they carry with them when they leave home, you have an ongoing role to play.

Start

Let everyone check in by sharing their answer(s) to one or both of these questions:

- What are some ways your parents passed along their spiritual beliefs and practices to you?
- Which, if any, of your parents' spiritual beliefs and practices remain part of your faith today?

Finish checking in by discussing your experiences with the between-sessions exercises and activities. What have you learned from completing these personal studies?

Watch Video (17:00 minutes)

Play the video segment for the sixth and final session (use the streaming video access provided with the study guide). As you watch, use the following video notes to record any thoughts or concepts that stand out to you.

- When you consider the faith of your children, what's the win? What are you hoping and praying for? Your *win* will determine your *role* in the development of your children's faith.

- What happens at *home* is far more catalytic than what happens at *church*. If your faith doesn't make a practical difference in your life, odds are it won't make a difference in your children's lives.

- Only you can demonstrate day by day, season by season what it looks like to live out your faith. If you want to pass along your faith, you will *always* have a role to play.

- **Emphasize a personal relationship with God.** Directing your children's attention to God's will, or plan for their lives, is an important first step in helping them develop a relationship with and accountability to their heavenly Father.

- Teach your children to **pay attention to their hearts**. In the Old Testament book of Proverbs, the author writes, "Above all else, guard your heart, for everything you do flows from it" (4:23).

- How do you teach them to guard their hearts? Regularly asking heart questions provides opportunities to talk. The questions you *most often* ask your children communicate what's *most important* to you and what you're convinced should be most important to them.

- Another way to cultivate your children's faith is by **praying as a family in every season**.

- **Be honest about your own faith journey.** For your children to have a faith of their own, it's imperative they understand how faith intersects with the real world.

- **Make church—the right church—a priority.** If you do, you and your kids will have the benefit of another adult or two reiterating at church what you're modeling and teaching at home.

- Don't let your faith get in the way of your relationships with your children. Parent with the relationship, not their faith, in mind. Remember, *relationship is influence.*

Group Discussion

As you consider what you just watched, use the following questions to discuss with your group members these ideas, their basis, and their application in your life.

1. How would you describe the win of helping your children develop a faith of their own? What or who has influenced your view of this win?

2. Do you agree that what happens at home influences your child's faith more than what happens at church? Why?

3. What do you consider a first step in helping your children know and relate to God and his plan for their lives? How have you implemented this step with your kids?

4. How often does your family pray together? How can you incorporate prayer more regularly and organically into your daily family life?

5. What are some ways you have taught your kids to pay attention to their hearts and what's going on inside them? How have you connected this to having faith?

6. Do you agree that your faith should not get in the way of a relationship with your children? Why or why not?

Process Your Parenting

Like so many other aspects of parenting, helping your children develop their own faith often depends on your views and practices related to it. Once again, there is no simple formula or guaranteed process by which you can ensure that your child matures into an adult with an active, vibrant faith. As you've likely concluded, so much of how you communicate your faith to your children happens in mundane, everyday moments. Regarding faith, what you *do* may speak louder than your words.

Drawing on the collective wisdom of the group, discuss your answers to the following questions with the goal of encouraging and inspiring one another as you help your children cultivate their own faith.

- What faith practices are regular, even routine, parts of your daily family life? What impact do they seem to be having on your children?

- What's one faith practice you stopped doing or overhauled when you realized it wasn't having the positive effect you desired?

- How do you see church attendance and participation contributing to your children's spiritual development? Has your church helped reinforce what you're trying to teach and model at home?

- As you look ahead to your children as adults, how do you want them to live out their faith? How would you describe the role you want faith to have in their adult lives?

Pray

As you conclude this last session, go around the group and share one important takeaway from this study. Share any personal prayer requests you would like others to pray about, both now and after this final session. Thank God for all he has shown you, taught you, and given you through this small group study. Ask for his continued blessings on each of you and your families as the group completes this time together.

Between-Sessions Personal Study

Now that you've completed all six sessions, use these final questions and exercises to help you reflect and evaluate your experience and all you've learned. Make sure you finish reading *Parenting* if you haven't already done so. As you will see in the following sections, you're asked to try to remain in touch with group members in order to continue encouraging, inspiring, and upholding one another on your respective journeys as parents.

Pause

Looking back over all you've learned and experienced, both in your group time and personal studies, begin this final personal study by reviewing your ideas about parenting. Focus on what's new, different, or unique in your view of parenting compared with before you started this study. Jot down what you especially appreciated from your time with the group, from reading the book, and from completing this video study. Feel free to make your own list, or use these prompts to get you started.

One way my view of parenting has changed is . . .

Perhaps my biggest takeaway from this entire study is . . .

The parenting tip I'm most excited about practicing right now is . . .

I am thankful for the group sessions because . . .

I believe I'm better equipped to parent since becoming intentional about . . .

Pursue

Never underestimate the role of prayer in parenting, especially where your children's spiritual lives are concerned. In times of stress, conflict, or crisis, you may naturally default to praying for your children. But as you know, praying consistently through all of life's daily ups and downs has a greater impact, both on your faith as well as your children's.

At some point in their lives, often as they transition into adulthood, your children may reject your faith and seemingly abandon interest in anything spiritually related. This is often a natural part of the process for developing a personal faith. You don't want your children to believe and practice a faith just because it's what you want. They must make it their own, and that frequently involves wrestling with God and struggling to follow the teachings of Jesus.

During this transition time, or on other occasions when your kids seem uninterested in matters of faith, make prayer your default response rather than pressuring them or trying to force them to comply. Trust that your prayers will be heard and answered, though perhaps not as quickly as you would like or even the way you might prefer. As a reminder to make prayer your first response as you parent, read the passage below and then answer the questions that follow.

> Jesus said to them, "Suppose you have a friend, and you go to him at midnight and say, 'Friend, lend me three loaves of bread; a friend of mine on

a journey has come to me, and I have no food to offer him.' And suppose the one inside answers, 'Don't bother me. The door is already locked, and my children and I are in bed. I can't get up and give you anything.' I tell you, even though he will not get up and give you the bread because of friendship, yet because of your shameless audacity he will surely get up and give you as much as you need.

"So I say to you: Ask and it will be given to you; seek and you will find; knock and the door will be opened to you. For everyone who asks receives; the one who seeks finds; and to the one who knocks, the door will be opened." (Luke 11:5–10)

• What role has prayer played in your parenting? How do you usually pray for your children?

• What needs and requests have you recently been praying for? What are your expectations about God's response to your requests?

• When have you prayed specifically for your children's needs and experienced God's solution, provision, or blessing? Did he answer your prayers gradually over time or more immediately?

- Read through the passage above once more and make it your prayer. Ask God to help you understand, appreciate, and practice prayer as part of being the parent you want to be.

Practice

Friendships and healthy community can provide enormous support through all the stages of the parenting journey. Think back on each of your group sessions and how each person contributed to your experience. Think about each group member and what you learned from them or appreciated about their contributions. Use the following questions to help you bring closure to this study even as your journey as a parent continues.

- What are some of the specific moments, people, and words from your group meetings for which you're particularly thankful?

- What surprised you most about your group experience during this study? What disappointed you?

- What will you take with you now that your group has concluded this study? How have you changed as a parent since starting these sessions?

- Which group member or members had the greatest impact on your experience? Which ones inspired you to be a better parent with their words, questions, prayers, and actions?

- Spend a few minutes praying for each member of your group and thanking God for who they are and how they impacted you during your time together.

- Finally, during the week after your group's final session, choose at least one other group member and send them a text or email or call to check in and let them know you are thinking about them and praying for them. If the group wants to continue meeting, consider inviting all your families to a potluck or cookout so you can get better acquainted.

Leader's Guide

Thank you for agreeing to lead a small group through this study. What you have chosen to do is valuable and will make a great difference in the lives of others.

The *Parenting Video Study* is a six-session study built around video content and small-group interaction. As the group leader, just think of yourself as the host of a dinner party. Your job is to take care of your guests by managing all the behind-the-scenes details so that when everyone arrives, they can just enjoy the time together.

As the group leader, you don't have to answer all the questions or reteach the content—the video, book, and study guide will do most of that work. Your job is to guide the experience and create an environment where people can process, question, and reflect—not receive more instruction.

Make sure everyone in the group gets a copy of the study guide. This will keep everyone on the same page and help the process run more smoothly. If some group members are unable to purchase the guide, arrange for people to share the resource with other group members. Giving everyone access to all the material will position this study to be as rewarding an experience as possible. Everyone should feel free to write in their study guides and bring them to group every week.

Setting Up the Group

As the group leader, you'll want to create an environment that encourages sharing and learning. A church sanctuary or formal classroom may not be as ideal as a living room because those locations can feel formal and less intimate. No matter what setting you choose, provide enough comfortable seating for everyone, and, if possible, arrange the seats in a semicircle so everyone can see the video easily. This will make transition between the video and group conversation more efficient and natural.

Also, try to get to the meeting site early so you can greet participants as they arrive. Simple refreshments create a welcoming atmosphere and can be a wonderful addition to a group study evening. Try to take food and pet allergies into account to make your guests as comfortable as possible. You may also want to consider offering childcare for those with children. Finally, be sure your media technology is working properly. Managing these details up front will make the rest of your group experience flow smoothly and provide a welcoming space in which to engage the content of *Parenting*.

Starting Your Group Time

Once everyone has arrived, it's time to begin the group. Here are some simple tips to make your group time healthy, enjoyable, and effective.

First, consider beginning the meeting with a short prayer, and remind the group members to put their phones on silent. This will ensure you can all be present with one another and with God. Then, give each person one or two minutes to respond to the questions in the "Start" section. You won't need much time in Session 1, but beginning in Session 2, people will likely need more time to share together and to enjoy getting better acquainted. Usually, you won't answer the discussion questions yourself, but you may need to go first a couple of times to set an example, answering briefly and with a reasonable amount of transparency. Also during the "Start" section, help the members who completed the personal studies debrief their experiences. Debriefing something like this is a bit different from responding to questions based on the video, because the content comes from the participants' real lives.

At the end of Session 1, invite the group members to complete the between-sessions personal studies for that week. Explain that you will be providing some time before the video teaching next week for anyone to share insights. Let them know sharing is optional, and it's no problem if they can't get to some of the between-sessions activities some weeks. It will still be beneficial for them to hear from the other participants to learn what they discovered.

Leading the Discussion Time

Now that the group is engaged, it's time to watch the video and respond with some directed small group discussion. Encourage all the group members to participate, but make sure they know they don't have to do so. As the discussion progresses, you may want to follow up with comments such as, "Tell me more about that," or, "Why did you answer that way?" This allows the group participants to deepen their reflections and invites meaningful sharing in a nonthreatening way.

Note that you have been given multiple questions to use in each session, and you do not have to use them all or even follow them in order. Feel free to pick and choose questions based on either the needs of your group or how the conversation is flowing. Also, don't be afraid of silence. Offering a question and allowing up to thirty seconds of silence is okay. It allows people space to think about how they want to respond and also gives them time to do so.

As the group leader, you are the boundary keeper. Do not let anyone (yourself included) dominate the group time. Keep an eye out for group members who might be tempted to "attack" folks they disagree with or try to "fix" those having struggles. These kinds of behaviors can derail a group's momentum, so they need to be steered in a different direction. Model active listening, and encourage everyone in your group to do the same. This will make your group time a safe space and create a positive community.

The group discussion time leads to a closing group or individual activity. During this time, encourage the participants to take just a few minutes to review what they've learned and write down two key takeaways. This will help them cement the big ideas in their minds as you close the session. Close your time together with prayer as a group.

Thank you again for taking the time to lead your group. You are making a difference in the lives of others and having an impact on the kingdom of God.

Parenting

Getting It Right

Andy and Sandra Stanley

Am I getting parenting right? Most parents, at any and every stage, find themselves asking this question.

Whether you're sleep deprived with a colicky newborn or navigating the emotional roller coaster of a teenager, parenting has its ups and downs, its confusion and clarity, its big blowups and small victories. And no matter our family makeup or our children's personalities, many of us experience anxiety over our children's futures and often fear making a mistake.

Andy and Sandra Stanley are no strangers to this feeling. As parents of three grown children and cofounders of North Point Ministries, they are seasoned experts on faith and parenting. Together they have spent decades counseling countless families, mentoring others, and learning from mentors of their own, all while leading one of the largest churches in the country.

In *Parenting: Getting It Right*, Andy and Sandra combine their experience and wisdom into a guide that helps readers understand and live by essential parenting principles. In an inviting, conversational approach that is both informative and accessible, the Stanleys help readers understand the most important goal in parenting and learn the steps to pursue it by:

- Learning the four distinct stages of parenting
- Clarifying the primary goal of parenting and developing a parenting orientation around that goal
- Identifying and adapting their approach—not their rules—to their children's distinct personalities
- Deciding on their shortlist of nonnegotiables and learning to stick to it

You don't have to constantly doubt if you're getting it right as a parent. Start here and feel confident about raising a healthy and happy family.

Available in stores and online!

Uncover the five key questions that can change everything about your decision-making process and rewrite the story of your life . . . one decision at a time.

In this six-session study, Andy Stanley helps you apply the principles in *Better Decisions, Fewer Regrets* to your life. The study guide includes video notes, group discussion questions, and personal study and reflection materials for between sessions.

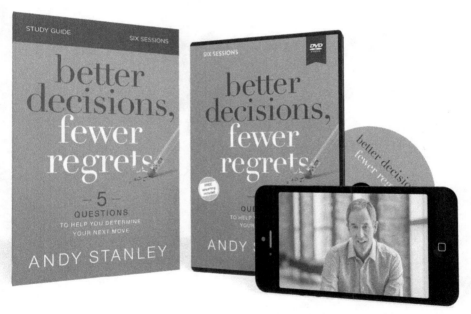

Study Guide
9780310126560

DVD with Free Streaming Access
9780310126584

Available now at your favorite bookstore, or streaming video on StudyGateway.com.

Harper*Christian*
Resources

CPSIA information can be obtained
at www.ICGtesting.com
Printed in the USA
JSHW010039170223
37754JS00006B/88

Design Disasters: t Designer, abulous Failures Lessons Learned

Edited by Steven Heller

12   11   10   09   08   5   4   3   2   1

Published by Allworth Press
An imprint of Allworth Communications, Inc.
10 East 23rd Street, New York, NY 10010

Cover design by James Victore, Inc.
Interior design by Shawn Hasto

ISBN-13: 978-1-58115-508-2
ISBN-10: 1-58115-652-9

Library of Congress Cataloging-in-Publication Data:

Design disasters : great designers, fabulous failures, and lessons learned / edited by Steven Heller.
     p. cm.
ISBN-13: 978-1-58115-652-2
ISBN-10: 1-58115-652-9
1. Designers--Psychology. 2. Failure (Psychology) I. Heller, Steven.

NK1520.D46 2008
745.4--dc22
                              2008015367

Table of Contents

Acknowledgments

Thanks to Tad Crawford, publisher of Allworth Press for being such a consistent champion of design writing and publishing. Also at Allworth gratitude goes to Bob Porter, Associate Publisher; Kate Ellison and Melanie Tortoroli, Assistant Editors; and Michael Madole, Publicist. James Victore has never failed to produce provocative covers for my Allworth Books, and I thank you for so many of them.

Of course, I appreciate the support of the contributors to this volume, but mostly Ralph Caplan, because without fail he rises to the call whenever a project beckons.

Finally, thanks to the School of Visual Arts for all their encouragement, particularly President David Rhodes, who has underwritten many of these Allworth projects, and to Lita Talarico, co-chair of the MFA Designer as Author program, who has always been a valued collaborator.

—SH

Intro-
duc-
tion

Designing Failure

By Steven Heller

Wikipedia has a very terse entry for failure that from my perspective as a connoisseur of failure is a total failure (which is both good and bad). The problem, however, is that the core definition used in this Wiki is pretty unsatisfying: In general, failure refers to the state or condition of not meeting a desirable or intended objective. It may be viewed as the opposite of success. For me, failure is such a deep mine of experience that one should expect considerably more depth than merely a few subsections devoted to "commercial failures" and "military disasters." Although there are links to such phenomena as Murphy's Law, which states, "things will go wrong in any given situation, if you give them a chance," and fiasco, "a complete or humiliating failure," nothing whatsoever is mentioned about failure as a design construct (or, for that matter, a design strategy). You'd think that design and failure would be a mother lode of a theme. Just look at how the world has been impacted by failed design—both positively and negatively. But that's not all: It is surprising that a subsection entitled "learning from mistakes" or "profiting from failure" is nowhere to be found, unless, of course, the Wiki interface design is so inadequate that I couldn't find it, which in either case is a failure—right?

This book is devoted to design and failure (and failure by design and failure with design and design failures (made) by designers). If I were the joking sort, I would just make the type from here on unreadable as an example of failed design. Frankly, I am certain the joke would fail because defining design failure is much more complicated than any such visual pun or technical glitch. What's more, I still want readers to read, so screwing around with the type provides no long-term functionality. Instead, I will try (although I may fail miserably) to discuss the reasons why a book on failure is valuable and essential, and in so doing touch on why failure is an essential part of any creative endeavor, particularly design—all kinds of design.

First, I mustn't fail to mention that it goes without saying that an awful lot of design success is actually rooted in or built on failure. In the best situations, failure is a trigger. But this is different from (difference) "trial and error," whereby a designer plays with forms until the perfect (or near perfect) one is achieved and actually results in something that will, as our Wiki states, "meet a desirable or intended objective." But many times what a designer thinks is perfect, and so releases to the world, is a flop. With luck, even this will provide a lesson for what not to do the next time or the time after that.

Failures come in many shapes and sizes. They are major and minor, although mostly they fall somewhere in between. Sometimes they are costly; other times not. Usually they go unnoticed, but occasionally they are highly publicized. One of the classic cases of design failure is the Ford Edsel automobile. Here's what Wikipedia has to say about it: "The Edsel was a make of automobile manufactured by the Ford Motor Company during the 1958, '59, and '60 model years. The Edsel [or E- (for experimental) car] was a make of automobile manufactured by the United States automobile industry." Almost immediately there was an adverse public reaction to the car's styling and conventional build, in part because Ford had earlier circulated rumors that led consumers to expect an entirely new kind of car when in fact this new one shared its bodywork with other Ford models. But it wasn't simply the false publicity that disappointed the public; Edsel's distinctive grillwork seemed grafted onto a more conventional form. Some felt that rather than being original, the car was the product of melding parts together. Although the styling (i.e. the design) was blamed, most experts were never certain why the car failed. So what lesson was learned? Never produce an Edsel again—although today it's a collector's item—or at least test test test until no doubts remain.

Design failures are often the result of misreading the public's needs and tastes (which is why so many businesses invest in testing in an effort to avoid failure). However, sometimes they occur when, for some curious reason or another, these issues are ignored entirely. Often it's called hubris, but sometimes it's called thinking ahead of the curve. Some failures are simply good ideas that come before their time. Other times failure is part of the evolutionary nature of things. One might argue that prehistoric man, like Homo Habilis and Homo Georgicus, was imperfect (and possibly a failure) in the design sense, so he evolved into Homo Erectus, which led to homo "us" (although it's possible "we" may not be the final stage in evolutionary design, either). The intelligent designers responsible for these beings had other lessons to learn, so prehistoric failure was a test. Indeed, failures are good when they lead to better outcomes.

As a wishful perfectionist, I am unnerved by the notion of failure. A failing grade, for instance, whether in school or on a *Cosmopolitan* magazine compatibility-with-your-mate test, is a black mark, not a hopeful sign. Learning to learn from failure is not instinctive. It takes intestinal fortitude not to be devastated by failure and then real soul-searching to find the proverbial silver lining. Still, I always tell students it is better to fail and succeed later because the former will result in a much more detailed critique. For students, failing should be a stepping stone. Yet, often the most valuable lesson derived from failure is the simple revelation that it's time to alter behavior—it is more useful to stop digging the bottomless pit and move on to something else. Failure can be a behavioral traffic light—stop or go.

So, enough of this self-motivational mumbo jumbo! What makes failure so compelling for designers—and decidedly for those who have contributed to this volume—is that it is so frequently the wellspring for greater experience. Here is a case in point that I experienced: Years ago, I packaged a children's book with Seymour Chwast (he designed it, I helped conceive and edit it) that was a three-dimensional interpretation of Charles Dickens's *A Christmas Carol*. The book was designed to be a proscenium stage that would ostensibly pop up when opened. Characters were on perforated sheets, and a script was included so that children could play along. Although the manufacture was complex, it was doable and the final printed sample was very impressive. However, when a box of final books was sent to us from the printer, we noticed that the spines were crushed. Since this was not a traditional brick-like book but rather a box in the shape of a book, the support for the spine was minimal and so crushed under the weight of other books. The book dealers refused to accept their shipments, citing damaged goods as the reason. So we were forced to reprint and insert a cardboard support in the spine, increasing the price of the book (which we absorbed) and reducing the profit margin to nothing. This was indeed a failure of some magnitude, which didn't turn into a success, but it did teach a lesson. Always anticipate that which should be anticipated. We were so wrapped up in the creative process—design, writing, illustration—that we neglected the fundamental production concerns. Of course, someone on the production side should have warned us, but the lesson from this failure is: Never entirely rely on others. Design is a totality; every piece impacts on every other piece, and a designer must control the process lest the process control you. Failures occur when the big picture is ignored.

Perhaps readers of this book have experienced something similar to the above—or maybe not. But I am sure that everyone has experienced (and, I believe most are willing to admit to) failure of some kind. The various experiences shared in this volume may resonate among many, or maybe you'll ask why something is considered a failure when on the surface it may seem like a success. Whatever the response—or however you use this book—the most important thing is to embrace failures as endemic to the design process, learn from them, and even enjoy them.

Learnng rom ailure

On Failure

By Allan Chochinov

For all the talk of the value of learning through failure, it is difficult to get the concept across if we continue to use the word "failure" in that sentence. People have a natural aversion to the term, and it is next to impossible to reclaim it for pedagogic purposes.

For all the talk of the value of learning through failure, what we really mean is that it is valuable to do something multiple times, learning lessons from each attempt and applying those lessons to subsequent versions. This is a tough bargain, requiring both patience and diligence, and not a little thick skin.

For all the talk of the value of learning through failure, it is in the rewards of persistence where the true lessons lie, and the lessons of persistence can only be learned by those who persist—a kind of chicken-and-egg conundrum that can never be solved save by those who, you guessed it, can tolerate failure.

For all the talk of the value of learning through failure, it is really the notion of iteration that we should be concentrating on. It is the repeated doing of a thing that makes it better—not unlike learning any skill—but this is a difficult thing to get across to designers. They are pleased to get a thing done even once, never mind multiple times.

For all the talk of the value of learning through failure, it is iteration that should be up on the marquee. But it is not so much the "teaching" of iteration that we're talking about; rather, it is the appreciation of iteration, and this requires a stern but empathetic taskmaster, first external, but in the end, from deep inside.

For all the talk of the value of learning through failure, the quest for perfection is what we're really talking about here. It is the doing and redoing of a thing that gets one close to the ideal—removing the extraneous and preserving the essential—ultimately driving something toward its elemental, rarefied state.

For all the talk of the value of learning through failure, it is the pursuit of success that fuels the fire. In trying to succeed at something, we are destined to miss the mark on occasion, but to say that every time we fall short of "success" we "fail" is like saying that every time we don't win a baseball game we lose one. Wait, I guess that is saying that.

For all the talk of the value of learning through failure, it is really humility at the heart of the matter. It takes guts to recognize when something isn't working and bravery to attempt to do it again. It is the calling on these emotional components that make "failure the best teacher," not the successful or less-than-successful completion of the task at hand.

For all the talk of the value of learning through failure, it is the concept of rigor that deserves the discourse. Although it is often the first gesture that, in the end, remains standing as the best, rigorous investigation through multiple variations, if not generating better alternatives, will, at the very least, confirm what was first best all along.

For all the talk of the value of learning through failure, it is difficult to get the concept across if we continue to use the word "failure" in that sentence. People have a natural aversion to the term, and it is next to impossible to reclaim it for pedagogic purposes.

Fail
Safe

By Debbie Millman

For most of my adult life, I followed a safe path. I remember the moment I began the journey in vivid detail: August 1983, the hot, muggy summer of Synchronicity and Modern Love. I stood on the corner of 7th Avenue and Bleecker Street in New York City wearing pastel blue balloon trousers, a hot pink v-neck tee shirt, and bright white Capezio Oxfords, a recent college graduate peering deep into my future, contemplating the choice between knowing and not knowing, between the secure and the uncertain, between the creative and the logical. I dreamt of being an artist and a writer, but inasmuch as I knew what I wanted, I felt compelled to consider what was "reasonable" in order to ensure my economic future. Even though I wanted what my best friend once referred to as "the whole wide world," I thought it was prudent to compromise. I told myself it was more sensible to aspire for success that was realistically feasible, perhaps even failure-proof. It never once occurred to me that I could succeed at having it all.

I look back twenty years later and try to soothe myself with this rationale: I grew up in an atmosphere of emotional and financial disarray; my response as a young woman was tenacious self-sufficiency. Since then, I have lived within a fairly fixed code of possibilities. I am not an artist; I am a brand consultant. I don't work alone painting canvases and sculpting clay in a cold and quiet studio; I work in a bustling skyscraper and create logos for fast food restaurants and packaging for mass-market soft drinks and salty snacks and over-the-counter pharmaceuticals. I am not profoundly unhappy with what has transpired in the subsequent years; most days I consider myself lucky that I have a fun, secure job and a fairly hefty paycheck. But I know deep in my heart that I settled. I chose commercial security over artistic freedom, and I can't help but wonder what life would be like if I had made a different decision on that balmy night back in the West Village.

I made a surprising realization over the years: I am not the only person who has made this kind of choice. Not by a long shot. I discovered these common, self-imposed restrictions are rather insidious, although they start out simple enough. We begin by worrying we aren't good enough, smart enough, or talented enough to get what we want; then we voluntarily live in this paralyzing mental framework rather than face it. Just the possibility of failing turns into a dutiful self-fulfilling prophecy. We begin to believe that these personal restrictions are, in fact, the fixed limitations of the world. We go on to live our lives, all the while wondering what we can change and how we can change it, and we calculate and re-calculate when we will be ready to do the things we really want to do. And we dream. If only. If only. One day. Some day.

Every once and a while, (often when we least expect it) we encounter someone more courageous, someone who chose to strive for that which seemed (to us) unrealistically unattainable, even elusive. And we marvel. We swoon. We gape. Often, we are in awe. I think we look at these people as lucky, when in fact luck has nothing to do with it. It is really all about the strength of their imagination; it is about how they constructed the possibilities for their life. In short, unlike me, they didn't determine what was impossible before it was even possible.

John Maeda once said, "The computer will do anything within its abilities, but it will also do absolutely nothing unless commanded to do so." I think people are the same—we like to operate within our abilities. But whereas the computer has a fixed code, our abilities are limited only by our perceptions. Two decades after determining my code, and fifteen years working in the world of branding, I am now in the process of rewriting the possibilities of what comes next. I don't know exactly what I will become; it is not something that I can describe scientifically or artistically. Perhaps it is a "code in progress."

In the grand scheme of a life, maybe (just maybe) it is not about knowing or not knowing, choosing or not choosing. Perhaps what is truly known can't be described or articulated by creativity or logic, science or art—but perhaps by the most authentic and meaningful combination of the two: poetry. As Robert Frost once wrote, "A poem begins as a lump in the throat, a sense of wrong, a homesickness, a love sickness. It is never a thought to begin with."

I recommend the following course of action for those who are just beginning their careers or for those, like me, who may be reconfiguring mid-way through: Listen to Robert Frost. Start with a big, fat lump in your throat, start with a profound sense of wrong, a deep homesickness or a crazy love sickness, and run with it. If you imagine less, less will be what you undoubtedly deserve. Do what you love, and don't stop until you get what you love. Work as hard as you can, imagine immensities, don't compromise, and don't waste time. Start now. Not twenty years from now, not two weeks from now. Now.

Failure: An Owner's Manual

By Ben Kessler

Received wisdom has it that "success has many fathers, but failure is an orphan." In reality, however, it isn't possible to separate oneself from one's failure forever. In one way or another, the disowned child will present itself and demand to be acknowledged. The acceptance of blame can be postponed indefinitely, even dodged altogether, but failure always returns to where it came from. You can either own up to it—learn to own it—or allow it to own you. The only way out of making this choice is never to commit an error.

Owning a failure means recognizing yourself in it. If the child metaphor used above doesn't work for you, try thinking of failure as a sort of split-off cell that, under close scrutiny, yields important information about your basic makeup. The closer you look, the more you'll learn about yourself as a designer and as a person. That isn't always true of successes, which become split over time among many fathers. Those things of yours that the world rejects speak volumes about the differences between you and others.

It's possible, of course, simply to store your failure somewhere out of the way and never look at it. You can recognize it as having something vaguely to do with you without trying to trace the story it tells. That kind of avoidance, though, can result in the unwitting repetition of the initial error and the replication of the failure. Before you know it, you could have any number of identical failures crowded into your house or apartment, their unheeded cries for attention growing louder and louder. If you want to avoid this, it's best to learn to live in the same room as your failure.

Know this also: Your failure doesn't disappear just because you learn from it. Failures may age, but they don't die. It would be unwise to allow yourself to forget about an old failure because it has become unobtrusive. Should you duplicate an aging failure, the original will be restored to its former vigor and will agitate alongside its newborn double.

Remembering and acting upon these warnings won't prevent your room from filling up with failures as you grow older. Having learned to swerve past one pitfall, you will inevitably tumble into another. The rooms of the successful and the rooms of the thwarted differ in the diversity, not the number, of their failures. Successful dwellings are distinguished by a democracy of failure. In them, failures from all across the spectrum of human experience teem in happy heterogeneity.

Designers who strive for success should prepare themselves for the challenges of doing creative work in the middle of an endless, polyglot failure party. Successful people, as we've seen, are fluent in the myriad languages of failure and take them seriously when they speak. But in order to add to their failure menagerie, the successful have to learn to shut out failure's voices when action is required. The cultivation of this selective listening is an art in itself.

I am not suggesting that you can expect to spend your entire life listening to failure. You will be happy to know that there are two conditions that can bring you protracted peace and quiet: the onset of old age and infirmity. Out of respect for mortality, failure falls silent when these conditions appear. Nonetheless, it lives on after us, as part of the wake we make when we pass through the world. After you leave the earth, your failures will remain, silent and unmoving, waiting imperturbably for your descendants to revive them.

From the Annals of Self-Delusion

By Robert Grossman

In 1987, the editors of *Forbes* magazine asked me to illustrate a special section they were preparing called "America's Richest Entertainers." Over the preceding twenty or so years, I had developed a satisfying career as a cartoonist and illustrator, doing the thing I had loved best from early childhood, the only thing I was remotely good at—drawing pictures—and actually getting paid for it. I made a decent living, owned a house and a car, sent my children to fancy private schools, and yet was comfortable with the notion that, while being an artist was fun and preferable to any kind of "real work" I might imagine doing, it was obviously no way to get rich.

The *Forbes* article led off with the fact that Elvis Presley continued to earn hundreds of millions of dollars, undeterred by being dead for many years. Then came my "Holy mackerel!" moment. High on the list with Elvis, Madonna, and Frank Sinatra was none other than Charles Schulz, who gave us Peanuts, and not far behind him were other creators of syndicated daily comic strips earning tens of millions per year. "Holy mackerel," I thought, "were you ever wrong"—not only is cartooning not "no way to get rich," but it has to be the best way to get rich anybody has ever invented—pure fun with pencil and paper, not requiring one's complete moral abasement, the mass enslavement of peons, or the destruction of scarce natural resources on a worldwide scale. "Hell," I thought, "I can do that." Clearly I owed my children and generations of unborn descendants my best effort at becoming a syndicated daily comic strip artist myself.

I resolved to do a cartoon a day for one month in order to get into the rhythm of my new career, send the resulting sample strips to a syndicate that would be thrilled to have me, and then just watch the tide of bucks roll in. I felt I needed a title character with an alliterative name and since mice, ducks, pigs, and woodpeckers were already taken, Marko Munk, a monkey with a prehensile tail would do nicely. My strip would be zany, with elements of science fiction and political satire including occasional animal characters based on real people. It would have a continuing story line, but each day's installment would end with a bang.

The work went easily, and I held strictly to my one-a-day-for-a month program. By the beginning of the fourth week, I was convinced that Marko Munk was the best thing I had ever done. As I mailed copies of it to editors of all the big cartoon syndicates, I mentally composed my acceptance speech for the Nobel Prize for Cartooning.

The reaction of the editors was unanimous and best expressed by the cartoon phrase, "What th—?" One man said simply, "I hate monkeys." Another offered that before I attempted such a thing again I had better learn how to draw. My girlfriend at the time, never known for diplomacy, said, "It stinks." The most astute analysis of my failure came from a friend, the artist Martial West-

ROBERT GROSSMAN

MARKO
MUNK

DAILY COMIC STRIPS · WEEKS 1 THROUGH 4

© R.G. 1987

burg, in the form of a cartoon: two kids in the subway studying the comics page of the Daily News. "How do you like Marko Munk?" one asks, and the other replies, "It be too cerebral for me."

And that was that. Needless to say, I was a little crestfallen. But I got over it. Almost.

The Power of Leaving Things Half Done

By Rob Trostle

It is impossible for me to finish anything. This is not based on laziness or an inability to bring projects to completion, but rather based on the idea that when something is finished, it is dead. The term "dead" is maybe a bit strong, but what I mean is the project no longer has the potential to adapt, to grow in an organic way, the way it does during the initial stages of designing. Throughout this part of the design process, the emergent form is directly based on the factors involved. What is the deadline? What is interesting right now? What typeface is appropriate? What is the budget? And most importantly, what is not working? These nonworking aspects are what keep the process open, dynamic, and productive. Once all the questions are answered, no possibility for generative failure exists. Nothing is left but a seamless narrative—the stymie of all growth possibilities.

I see seamless narratives as disingenuous. It is the same feeling I had after a visit to the Royal Gorge Bridge in Colorado as a child. We drove for hours passing a multitude of billboards promising unparalleled beauty, a really deep gorge (Would we be able to see the bottom?), and a great gift shop. However, we experienced it all in roughly ten minutes and left feeling a little taken aback. Obviously, this is the stratagem of the tourist trap, but in many ways, it is also the tactic of the seamless narrative. I find no room for me within either situation. Being told what I am experiencing leaves no way to make it mine. The visions I had in the car of scrambling around the red rock looking for secret caves where some bandits had hidden treasure were a far cry from what I actually did, which was to just look at the gorge—from a distance. In fact, the gift shop was the closest thing to a real experience. Buying something was my desperate attempt to make a connection to that place.

But what happens when room exists for each individual to complete the experience on their own terms (and not in the gift shop)? Although this sounds relatively simple, I have found it to be an incredible challenge. In one project, I designed an environmental signage system and web site to encourage people to explore the city of New Haven and document their journey online. I created (what I thought was) an open system allowing a new experience of the city each time they went exploring. It was possible to start anywhere and end anywhere. I was looking to reproduce the spontaneity and creativity of a soccer game in which the possible combinations between players and ball are infinite. What I failed to realize, however, is that the players possess the creativity, not the ball. Unfortunately, I was treating pedestrians like the ball—forcing them here and there under the pretense of an open system. I believe one critic summed it up by asking,

"You want me to want to wander around the city, and to do it on your terms?"

"Um, yeah, does that work for you?"

Obviously, that did not work out so well, but I did come to the conclusion that it is better for design to ask rather than tell, even better to simply create potential rather than ask. This allows each individual to come to the design on his own terms and does not demand he interact at all. But how to accomplish this was up in the air until I was asked halfway through my stint at graduate school whether I was trying to fail. If I was trying to fail, I was told, I should at least get serious about it. From this I started to think about my future, for one thing, and whether I would finish grad school. But, I also thought about failure to finish as a way to create life for a project beyond the design process.

I am in the throes of trying to implement this strategy— failing on a regular basis to finish, leaving projects in various states of completeness, and measuring each step I take to uncover exactly what creates the most potential for an ongoing life. Has this proved successful? Has it proved productive? Am I still in grad school?

My Hack Career

By Marian Bantjes

The first thing I did wrong was fail to get a proper education in design. Ten years as a typesetter served me well for typography, but when I foolishly started my own business without ever having worked in color or with images and having no idea what happens at a printer's, I set myself up for an endless string of traumas. Arrogantly pioneering seemed brave to me at the time, but I now wince at my needless self-isolation as I practiced a profession I knew nothing about, oblivious to what was happening in the world of design during one of its most interesting periods—the 1990s.

I probably should have told my business partner that I hated the name she proposed for our company. This would at least have prevented the confession five years later, during a staff meeting, that I was so embarrassed by the name "Communication by Design" that I wouldn't tell people what it was when I met them. We changed it shortly thereafter to "Digitopolis"—a name I never felt we fully lived up to.

Additionally, it was an incredibly foolish decision to work on PCs, leaving us largely unsupported in a Mac-centric environment. Service bureaus and printers were openly hostile to our files, relieved only that we used Quark and Type 1 fonts and not Corel-Draw and TrueType but quick to blame any problem—however unlikely—on our files.

After wooing one of our first clients with some impractically sparse poster design, my first job on press involved eighteen hours ('til 4 a.m.) trying to get film run at an uncooperative service bureau, followed by my first duotone (in purple and black) turning out a decidedly funereal brochure for our weeping client. A follow-up brochure—my first in full color—was printed on a low-grade web press and resulted in lurid colors that shifted radically in tone from page to page. The client fired us shortly after, with the memorable words "Coming here is worse than going to see the dentist." Ouch.

Seemingly slow to learn from my mistakes, I continued experimenting with duotones for various clients, and such experimentation almost always resulted in images that were either too dark or of dubious tone. We were saved from reprinting one disastrous project, printed on uncoated paper, in which the duotones were too dark and the grayscale images washed out and too light, only by the fact that my business partner was sleeping with the client's business partner. Phew! I suppose there was some compensation for regularly being referred to as "the girls."

Although my partner eventually stopped negotiating design services for cases of beer, it seemed to take us many years before even approaching fair market rates for our work. I can remember being outraged over another designer's fee for producing province-wide phone book covers based on our Web site design, which was approximately forty times what we proposed charging. They got the contract. It wasn't until many years later that I understood the concept of usage fees.

The first logo I ever designed, after about fifty proposed sketches, was set in Centaur, of all things, with a gradient behind (perhaps I was ahead of my time). I think they fell in love with the swash V in Vancouver, which I developed into a cheesy monogram for them to stamp all over things (including enlarged and grayed out behind text, naturally). Another early logo also employed a swash V (custom), this time paired with Scala Sans Italic. It was lopsided, aligned with nothing, and impossible to work with, causing no end of trouble in every layout. It looked like shit centered, flush left, or flush right. However, the client loved it and wouldn't hear of changing it, so I was forced to work with my own failed design for six years.

Our first Web site, for the province's telephone company, was black—the impracticalities of which became quickly apparent, and resulted in a redesign (ours) a few months later; our first trade show display would have been great had it not been for the sagging, hand-painted backdrop; and our first store included changing-room curtains so short that customers were afraid to use them.

My bookish, well-crafted design aesthetic kept us many long-term clients, and we had our share of nightmarish clients and experiences, which never seemed to go away, although we became better at recognizing the early warning signs. But our real troubles grew internally while we continued to look externally for the causes and cures. Mostly, my partner and I believed we were too weak to deal with our clients, our staff, and each other. This led to the hiring of a "CEO": a former client who had terrified us with her hard-nosed approach in business meetings. My partner imagined our CEO would control our staff and play "bad cop" to our clients, I imagined that our CEO would control my partner, and we both imagined she would bring in new business.

That our new CEO didn't like our company look and required her own (redesigned) business cards was warning sign number one. The second sign was during a public function, when she expressed an inability to meet with strangers, thus proving that we had invited a third insecure woman into our fold. So much for getting new business. Where she had once terrified us, she now terrified our staff and the clash in corporate culture was disastrous, culminating in the firing of one of our employees (a sweet but incompetent designer who we had been completely incapable of firing ourselves), which was executed in the coldest and most corporate manner and which I feel guilty about to this day (despite suspecting that he left with my personally autographed copy of *The Elements of Typographic Style*.) The fallout of alienation nearly destroyed the fragile ecosystem of our company. My partner and I fired our CEO shortly thereafter and continued our struggles with each other.

It was the day my partner said that she had absolutely no interest in design, and she could be selling soap for all she cared that I realized how very wrong things had gone and how obvious it was that our partnership, our friendship, and our business was finally over. It took still another year before she bought me out and one more poisonous year of contract work for my former company before I left nine years as a graphic designer behind me and moved on to something more engaging between myself and the world. I had hundreds of pieces of mediocre work behind me, an armful of good work, a handful of excellent work but nothing exceptional to show for my career in design. It's difficult for me not to think of the entire thing—and a quarter of my life—as a complete failure. Although I know I learned much that would carry me forward, I often wonder whether a good four years in school wouldn't have served me better. Certainly it would have given me more in some respects, although not as much in life and business experience. I'm resigned to concede that these failures are valuable in learning and growing, and I'm hopeful that I wouldn't be who and what I am today were it not for the time spent floundering and following so many false leads and dead ends.

Portrait of the Artist as a Young Ulcer

By Rick Meyerowitz

I sat down at the long table with my Americano and a muffin the size of my brain. It may well have been my brain I was getting ready to eat; I was in no condition to judge. The last few hours hadn't come into focus for me yet. Maybe they never would. The white-bearded fellow across the table appeared to be observing me with some amusement. That's the problem with these communal tables, I thought. A person can't just stare into his coffee alone; he has to share the experience with strangers. I imagined jumping up and stabbing him with the plastic knife I was holding. Instead, I began sawing away at the muffin.

The two women to my right were chattering about their shoes: the shoes they were wearing and the shoes they were going to wear. One had a nasal voice; the other spoke in a screech. It's possible, I thought, that if their voices could be focused on the table in alternating waves of sound, they could cut it in half more quickly than I could saw through this muffin.

I sipped some coffee and dribbled a little on my shirt. What time did Maurice text me? Was it 9 a.m.? Funny, I don't know that I've actually spoken with him at all in the last two years.

It's all texting and email. Some agent, Maurie Schlick. When we met three years ago, he was young and smart and full of energy. He repped six illustrators and a photographer. I liked being part of his small group. Now the little "Maurice Agency" has become "Schlick-Art," and he reps 365 illustrators and photographers. As he says in his blog, "One for each day, and 366 in leap years."

I read his message with some interest. Why wouldn't I? I am starved for decent work these days.

"Lissen Kiddo: I gt sumthng for U up at Oblivimova, Ramaswaran, Gurdymukmohammodov, Patamarapippan, & Wu. Call Jugdish Berenstain NOW - unless U r 2 bizy doing nuthng - hah hah hh. Lissen, U call im. Don't fuggup ths job like last 1. I hve efuf trgedy in my life. Do I hve 2 remind U my grndfthr lived thru th holocust? Lissen, Maurie"

I didn't need a reminder. He did live through the holocaust, but in Milwaukee, where Maurie's German Catholic grandfather made hooch for the Capone mob before opening a bar down on the docks near Kazubes Park.

I phoned Jugish at the agency and left a message. He e'ed me from his BlackBerry a short while later.

"Dear Artist: Glad to be working with you. Love your work. Big job. Maybe a whole campaign. Don't have much money. We'll make it up to you. Need it by lunch today. Send sketches. JB"

It lacked the personal touch, but the layout was attached. It was an ad for a new drug, Polysyllablecine (Wookamookablabbadine). The headline was "Don't Ask Your Doctor. Trust Us!" Under the headline was a rough sketch of a man who appeared to be asleep on a cloud while a devil figure stood on his chest plunging a pitchfork into his abdomen. The man's expression seemed calm. I wondered what the drug was supposed to do—tranquillize you while you were mugged by a demon? Maybe it was a heartburn thing. Truth was I didn't care. I had two hours till it was due.

I opened Photoshop and began to draw. In ten minutes I had the sketch I wanted and e-mailed it to Jugdish. I heard back from him right away.

"Hey Artist. Good work. Can't use as is. Man looks dead. Nose needs shortening like an inch so we don't think he's Jewish. Shoes are wrong. Suggest sandals. Cloud looks like a cotton ball. Demon also looks Jewish. Suggest horns be removed and maybe he's wearing shorts and baseball cap backwards or something. But you're the artist. Make my day! The J. Man."

I tried a little yogic breathing waiting until my pulse settled. Then I gave it another shot, incorporated all his suggestions, and sent it off.

"Hey! Got the revise here in cab on way to meeting. Something wrong with man. Now he looks like he's an Arab. Demon still looks Jewish. Lose the tail or client will shit! Suggest making demon purple instead of red. Pitchfork can be a garden hose and he's waking guy up with water. Cloud too cottony: more cloudlike. How about adding a dog? You the MAN! JB"

I read it and thought, "Did I just have a mini-stroke, or does this not make any sense at all?" It occurred to me I should drop this job like a hot burrito. Then I thought of the trip to Paris my girlfriend and I were going to make, and my mortgage, and what Maurie would say. So I stared at a photo of the Dalai Lama until the vein in my neck stopped pounding, then I did another sketch and hit send.

"Yo. Can't spend much time. Am in limo with client on

way to wine tasting extravaganza. Think we're moving in right direction. Whole thing might work if we pull ol' switcheroo & have man plunging pitchfork into chest of devil who is now wearing overalls. Man should also have gun in other hand & look like Arnold but not exactly. We don't want to get sued by the state of California. Cloud should be yellow and shaped like a banana. Love the dog but he looks Chinese. Can you give him something to do—like play an accordion? Almost there, baby! Big J."

A cornered man will do anything to escape. I understand rats will gnaw off their own legs if they have to. I was out on a limb and ready to start chewing it off. I'll admit to some whimpering as I worked, but the rest of the time remains a blur. The sketch? Finished. Sent. The doubts? Many. The big surprise? Jugdish wrote immediately to tell me it was perfect. I should do it and e-mail it to him ASAP.

The guys who created Photoshop are gods. I finished the illustration in record time and sent it off at noon on the button, with this note.

"Dear Jugdish: Here it is. I'm sorry we had to go through so many sketches, but what the heck, the creative process, right? I hope the client likes it and appreciates me turning it around so quickly for him. I really look forward to seeing the finished ad. I think it may be an award winner, and as long as it doesn't run in California we won't be sued, don't y'think? Thanks. RM"

I was putting things away and thinking about taking myself out for a well-deserved lunch when I heard the ping of an arriving e-mail.

"Hey Arty. Sorry about this, but the client felt my comp caught the feel of what they were looking for just a bit better than

your finished art. I spoke with Maurice, and there'll be the usual 10% kill fee, but accounting is still working through the 1999 bills, so it may take a while. Well, gotta sign off. I'm leaving for Paris on the client's jet. We're going to brainstorm a European campaign. You should see the legs on these models! Hang in there! Juggy" Attached was the finished ad with the headline and his rough pencil-sketch below. The client may have been right. It didn't look half bad.

The mail pinged again. It was Maurie.

"Lissen: U blu ths job. U wanna work 4 kill fees, gt a job in slaughterhouse! Get it? Hah hah hh. Lissen: 60% of what U make wouldn't keep my parakeet happy, let alone my wife & my girlfriend. Lissen: There r plenny othr illustrators out there. Do I have to draw U a picture? Hah hh. Lissen, Maurie"

"Hey! Cranberry." I looked up, startled. "What? What'd you say?"

"You've thrown a cranberry on me," said the old guy across the table. "You were waving your plastic knife around and talking to yourself. One of the cranberries from your muffin landed in my beard."

"Uhhh, sorry," I mumbled.

"I can relate to what you were talking about," he said. "I was an illustrator myself. Got my start back in the 60s. Even though you were mumbling, I recognized elements in your story from my own career. I had plenty of success, but I also had a failure or two."

"That so," I said. I looked around for an escape route. The women had moved to a table by the window. They seemed more subdued now, staring into their salads and trying not to look my way. It was just me and the old guy at a table that sat sixteen. I noticed people were waiting on line for tables rather than sitting with us.

"Yep, I got a story about this one job you might be interested in. I was doing illustrations before computers or scanners. We didn't even have FedEx back then; we painted on paper with brushes, and delivered work ourselves or we used messengers. We knew the art directors personally. This one time, back in '78, I did a painting for a movie poster. Took me four days. It was some amazing piece of art, measured about 30 x 40. I was sure this would be the job that made me famous. So I called for a messenger. Guy named Dexter showed up on his bike. I'll never forget it. He only had one leg …"

"Yeah, yeah," I said standing up, brushing crumbs off my chest and throwing some money on the table. "I have to get back to work. Besides, last thing I need to hear is another damn story about failure." I walked to the door and opened it. It was fall. Leaves were blowing down Spring Street. I turned around. The old illustrator was struggling to brush something from his beard. He looked up at me. "A one-legged bike messenger? You got to be kidding me," I said. And I walked out into the street.

The Language
of Failure

ge

Failure Is an Occasion for Mixing Meta-phors

By David Barringer

Failure is relative. It's relative to the perspective of the judge. It's relative to time. It's relative to the moment in time—a moment in the process, in the project, in the life—that is arbitrarily frozen and extracted and weighed in the scale of whim. Failure is the gritty feel of being alive and alone, hurtling through time and space to our absolute end. Success is just the label on the diorama.

Success is only possible to the extent you believe your life is a figure of speech.

Failure is relative. Today's bloom is tomorrow's wilt. With age, things grow into their opposites. Looking back, I see my success sour into failure, and my failure glint in the rays of reappraisal. Failure is a snap verdict shouted from a passing limo. Success, too, is a garbled shout from behind a tinted window. Or did they shout something else? Quick, claim my success. Plant the little toothpick flag of hope in my sandwich triangle. Success! It's delicious because the little red paper pennant says so. Or, as my grandmother used to say when serving three-day-old leftovers, "Quick. Eat it before it goes bad."

I could always taste it going bad as it sat there on my tongue.

*

The game is rigged. Success or failure depends on the definitions, which change over time. It's a success because I met the deadline; because I met the budget; because I made someone happy; because I got to keep the blue I wanted; because I got paid; because I redid the whole thing, and surprise, surprise, I made it better. But give it a week, and then it's a failure because I made a typo in the rush to meet the deadline; because the someone I made happy has changed their mind; because my blue looks sickly under mercury-vapor lights; because the check bounced; because my changes improved the work but now, looking back, I realize it just looks slicker, not better, and slicker means viewers can ignore it and move on, and well, that's failure.

Failure is relative when I internalize the ever-changing judgments of others, especially those others with no stake in the matter. Am I fishing for compliments with all my effort? Is that what I'm after, sweet nothings I can replay in the iPod of my imagination as I drift into dreamland? Hey, that's great. We love it. It's pretty good. It's fine. It's workable. A solid start. Once I realize I can marshal rationalizations to justify the relative success or failure of pretty much anything, then I need to stick closer to the world as seen through my eyes, as changed by my hands.

Why do I work? Who am I becoming? These are the questions whose lifelong answers blunt the slings and arrows of outrageous fortune. I have made mistakes that cost tens of thousands of dollars. I have made boring things, detestable things, trite, derivative, and sloppy things. I made changes the client wanted, but I made them to the nth degree, and the client said, "This is design with a vengeance." I smiled because sometimes failure is the only self-respecting way to respond to others' expectations. But then I had to suck it up and change it all. I have stared with the vanity of Narcissus at the monitor of my magnificence only to witness the poverty of its printed form and recoil in horror and shame. Man, what a piece of crap I just made. Please, let me dig a hole. Let me start again. I can do better.

Or maybe I can only ever do more. I can't succeed. I can't fail. I can't go back. I can just do more.

*

Success depends on giddy self-delusion, and I never feel successful because I know I have merely managed, for the time being, to keep my errors a secret. Success can only be perceived in the symbols of others' achievements, in the way I ascribe to the soaring hawk an air of superiority rather than the ache of hunger.

*

Before I correct a mistake, I imagine it as intentional.

*

Then I imagine all my intentions as mistakes.

*

Designers should never abort their wild ideas in utero. Let them be born. Designers have all sorts of difficult children. Some of their names are Convention, Tedium, and Tired. Some of their names are Gimmick, Bullshit, and Fraud. Try as you might to raise them right, you'll never get to name your own kids.

*

My compromises in life, work, and love are not made for survival. They are decisions by which I define the good life to myself. If I screw up, I admit it and try something else. The longer I blame others, the more irreversibly I compromise myself. The more I cling to my past failures, the less strength I have to reach out for the next inevitable failure. It is not by obedience but by intention that I define myself. I must want and act on that want. I may otherwise survive, but I will be a waste.

*

If others consider my work a success, they are granting a kind of posthumous recognition: The work of that art is over; the creator I was when I made it, I am no longer. I need so badly to work that working badly doesn't matter. That's the test. Not posterity. My world is already ending. I decay; my work decays; all mass recycles into energy, reforms into mass. And my great-great-grandkids won't give a shit either. I don't even know what my great-great-grandparents did for a living. I keep working because it hurts too much not to.

*

It always helps to know that it's normal to regard one's own work as both worthless and worthwhile. I have to reassure myself that it's worthwhile enough to have done it and yet not good enough to prevent me from continuing to improve and experiment.

The feeling never goes away, that I am somehow wasting time. I just learn to ignore it. Putting my work out there is like a mood-enhancing drug. The euphoria is intense but fleeting. Still, it keeps me from going crazy and driving my friends and family completely nuts. I still drive them nuts; they drive me nuts, but this is all life stuff, and I do what I need to do to make my life worthwhile while minimizing the collateral emotional damage I wreak on other people.

*

Emotionally, I remain an ambivalent wreck about my work. My insecurity compels me to revisit my little creations, review them, reassure myself that they aren't devastatingly terrible. I am not always reassured. Living with my work long outlasts midwiving its production. I love the power and control of writing and designing books and magazines, but I now understand why certain artists destroy their work. Better to die in obscurity than live in humiliation. This is a victim's sentiment, and I overcome it by working. Better to live with hope than die with regret. There is always the sense, however, that what I've done just isn't good enough. This grander failure hangs over my head, haunts my dreams, itches me like a rash. Supposedly that's why I keep working, but I think my belief in my grand failure is really a self-imposed discipline in disguise, born of necessity. I need to work, so I reject what I've done and draw another line in the sand and say to myself, "Try it again. One more time. This'll be the one!" I think it would be awful to think I've already done my best work, and all I need to do now is hunt in Africa or drink until the movie's made or annoy family and friends with my limp sorry lingering presence. I always rework everything, but I ride the waves of my output like I'm afraid it's the last time I'll ever be able to get anything done. Then, like some kind of manic-depressive, I hate it all. I stop. I get moody. Everything sucks, and nothing is worth doing. I wait for this to pass. It has every time so far.

One day it won't.

tumbling Is he Cost of Ioing Busi- ess

By Ralph Caplan

If we should fail—
> We fail!

But screw your courage to the sticking place,
And we'll not fail.
Macbeth

Someone is bound to say, or to already have said, that failure is the new success. They won't be far wrong. Pop psychology shelves are already loaded with books recounting how the authors flopped their way to fulfillment. A precursor of sorts was Jo Coudert's 1965 best-seller, *Advice from a Failure*. Forty years later a typical title is *We Got Fired! And It Was the Best Thing That Ever Happened to Us*, by the motivational author Harvey Mackay. Since the authors, the case-study subjects, and the endorsers of such books are all successful (The jacket of *We Got Fired* has a photo of, and blurb from, Donald Trump) failing seems to be a habit best indulged in moderation. Not even motivational gurus write books about chronic losers.

As trends go, this is one of the more benign. Even so, like all trends, it is subject to immediate disappearance. Trends—superficial, simplistic, ephemeral, rooted in fashion—come and go. In design, however, failure as a means to success is a constant. It comes with the territory and stays there, where it has a crucial part to play.

You can't learn from mistakes without making some. That self-evident dictum applies to life generally but is particularly applicable to professions that traffic in discovery. Both the lives and work of the most celebrated contributors to science, invention, and design—Edison, Marconi, Fuller—were a series of failures that culminated in triumph.

Our most widely publicized design failures—NASA's Columbia, Challenger, and Apollo 1, the New Orleans levees, Boston's Big Dig, the Tacoma Narrows Bridge, Ford's Edsel, Coca Cola's New Coke—dramatize the extent to which failure is inextricably tied to the design process. The phenomenon is examined and clarified by Henry Petroski in *Success Through Failure: The Paradox of Design*. The author of several wonderfully illuminating books about how things work and why they so often don't, Petroski reveals failure in design to be less of a paradox than paradigm.

Design practice depends so much on the functional inevitability of failure that it requires an instrument devised largely for the purpose of making mistakes. Namely, the model. Models and mockups are practice arenas for making mistakes in order not to make them in costlier venues later on.

The celebrated Gossamer Condor (1977) and Gossamer Albatross (1979) moved human-powered flight from fantasy to reality. In lectures and films explaining how they were developed, inventor Paul MacCready stressed the importance of test crashing. His design team's modus operandi was to identify the point of failure and keep backing away from it. They put a prototype into the air until it crashed, then reduced the weight incrementally and flew the plane until it crashed again. They kept doing this until the plane didn't crash, at which point they began adding weight until they determined the heaviest fuselage able to make the flight.

You can't argue with success, they say; but you can argue with failure. And if you do, it invariably argues back convincingly and instructively. The rewards are often astonishing. This may be what the management guru Tom Peters had in mind when he said, "Nothing is more important or beneficial for individuals or organizations than screwing up." But how to screw up productively? Designer Laurie Rosenwald, who calls herself "the World's Most Commercial Artist," runs a workshop on "making mistakes on purpose." When she invited me to join it, I argued that blundering is a skill in which I need no further training. That is true enough, but it was a smartass answer. If we can learn from mistakes, I suppose we can learn how to make the ones most worth learning from.

"Failure is not an option," we are told repeatedly, and in a sense it almost never is. An option is by definition an act of choice, and failure is rarely the choice of choice. But it is a possible outcome, and the prospect can be frightening. At best the results are embarrassing; at worst they may be tragic. But failure is most damaging when unacknowledged, for the cost continues to grow as the likelihood of correction is diminished. The fear of failure is pernicious and, as Oscar Hammerstein said of race prejudice, has to be carefully taught. Watching my grandchildren, or anyone else's, I can't help noticing that one reason they learn so quickly is that they start with no self-consciousness. Failure, which small children encounter at every turn, frustrates them, but it does not embarrass them. For toddlers, and designers, stumbling is just the cost of doing business. Alan Murray, inventor of the Murray Space Shoe, made a pair of ice skates for me, then taught me how to skate. "The trick," he explained, "is to keep falling and catching yourself on one knee." Sometimes you don't manage to catch yourself until one knee or more has already hit the ice, but the system works, and that seems to be pretty much how kids learn to walk. As they grow older they develop what Adam and Eve got as a gift from God—a sense of shame that impedes learning for life.

Unworkable ideas are to be avoided when possible, but although acting on them is dangerous, confronting them is not. Remember brainstorming? That cheap and easy formula for solving problems was heralded as a key to creativity and fell out of favor soon enough when it turned out not to be. But it had its uses, and still has. The hype did focus attention on creativity, and the technique did demonstrate the utility of letting even dumb ideas come to the surface. I once attended a brainstorming session for designers, led by a facilitator who asked the group to call out all the ideas we could think of on a given subject. We were instructed to withhold any consideration of how nonsensical or outrageous an idea might be, and as each idea was expressed, the facilitator wrote it on a blackboard. I remember one serious and accomplished designer who was temperamentally unable to play the game. As soon as a bad idea (as they almost all were) was proposed, he argued fiercely against putting it on the blackboard at all. When it did appear, he attacked it with a battery of reasons, almost certainly valid, why it wouldn't work. But on a blackboard faulty ideas are harmless and potentially useful. He simply could not stand to see mistakes displayed, even in the ephemeral medium of chalk.

How do we even measure failure? Like so many other

experiences, it depends on whose ox is gored. The last words of
the health food activist Adele Davis are reported to have been, "I
failed!" What she apparently meant, if the quote is accurate, was
that, despite a lifetime of preaching nutritional virtue, she herself
got no further than the age of seventy.

In "Musee des Beaux Arts," a poem about Breughel's painting of Icarus falling from the sky, Auden reflects on the relativity of
failure:

> ... the ploughman may
> Have heard the splash, the forsaken cry,
> But for him it was not an important failure

Of course the fall of Icarus was itself a design failure, at-
tributable to faulty material specification. Daedelus made the wings
out of wax, which melted in flight. But the fault could as fairly be
blamed on flawed piloting: Icarus, who flew the mission, ignored
his father's warning and soared too close to the sun. Design, that
most human of pursuits, is inescapably prone to human error.

Failing, Failing, and Still Sailing

By Richard Saul Wurman

The winds of Puget Sound twisted, contorted, and destroyed the
Tacoma Narrows Bridge but also promoted urgent and exacting
aerodynamic research that ultimately benefited all forms of steel
construction. Beauvais Cathedral was built to the limit of the technology in its day, and it collapsed, but subsequent cathedrals made
use of its failure.

Who's to know where any technology ends if its limits are
not stretched? The machines of the world's greatest inventor, Leon-
ardo da Vinci, were never built, and many wouldn't have worked
anyway, but he was trying solutions where no man knew there were
even problems. Clarence Darrow became a legend in the courtroom
as he lost case after case, but he forced re-evaluations of contempo-
rary views of religion, labor relations, and social dilemmas.

Edwin Land's attempts at instant movies (Polarvision) absolutely failed. He described his attempts as trying to use an impossible chemistry and a nonexistent technology to make an un-manu-

facturable product for which there was no discernible demand. This created the optimum working conditions, he felt.

> My play was a complete success. The audience was a failure.—Ashleigh Brilliant

An Ode to Error

These people understood, tolerated, and even courted failure. They were alternately exhilarated, confident, and scared to death, but they didn't perceive failure as a stigma. They were able to say, "Sure, that didn't work, but watch this."

> He's no failure. He's not dead yet.—William Lloyd George

They saw failure not as a sign of defeat but as a prelude to success. Failure to them was a stage or step to be understood and then used to best advantage—a delayed success. They embraced failure and manipulated it as a creative agent to drive their work. Their lives were failure-success cycles. Their submarines sank, their rockets exploded, their domes collapsed, their serums didn't work. But they documented their mistakes, they tried something else, then something else, and then something else again.

> Failure is the condiment that gives success its flavor.—Truman Capote

From the artist's studio to the scientist's laboratory, for the satisfaction of a problem solved or a fortune gained, those who seek to live their dreams and to conquer the new or simply to challenge the status quo all risk failure.

Buckminster Fuller built his geodesic domes by starting with a deliberately failed dome and making it "a little stronger and a little stronger…a little piece of wood here and a little piece of wood there, and suddenly it stood up." He edged from failure to success.

> There has never been a time in the industry where there are more opportunities but such a lack of human capital," laments high tech headhunter David Beirne. "The talent is not there to populate all the companies that have sprung up. So a lot of guys who have made mistakes are getting in on the opportunities. A lot of sins are being forgiven.—*Forbes*, "Bouncing Back" (July, 1997)

A television program on "The Mystery of the Master Builders," part of the Nova series, made reference to how architects learned from mistakes to create some of the world's most beautiful Gothic cathedrals.

Builders of Notre Dame in Paris discovered that wind velocity increases with elevations, causing greater stress to taller buildings. "Pressures at the top of Notre Dame were much greater than anyone had foreseen," said the show's narrator. "The builders here had pushed into unknown territory. They faced new challenges, made mistakes, and devised new solutions. Notre Dame established the fashion for flying buttresses, but it was a fashion forged by necessity." And it was forged by trial and error. These discoveries led to the addition of flying buttresses to the cathedral at Bourges, France, which was not originally designed to have them.

But most of us equate failure with inadequacy or rejection. Failure suggests a shame to be borne in secret. Mistakes in school, on the job, or in social milieus are the switches with which we beat ourselves.

A major form of information anxiety exists because of the fear of failing to understand or of admitting a lack of understanding. Assimilating information means venturing into the realms of the new and unknown in order to come to understand them.

> Every strike brings me closer to the next home run.—Babe Ruth

With any new undertaking, the risk of failure increases. Some people shun new information and new technology to avoid the risk. Others persist despite their fears, but the burden of their fear of failure will make the acquisition of the new information that much more difficult.

Perhaps if we kept in mind that many extraordinary people expect failure, we wouldn't fear it so much and could begin to learn how to use it.

Proper Management of Failure Breeds Success

> ...In the high tech industry, failure is a prized, not a scorned, offense. Along Philadelphia's Main Line, on Wall Street, or in the Motor City, the executive who flops gets driven out and often becomes unemployable. But in Silicon Valley, failure is an everyday event. There's little (if any) stigma attached to a washout. Failing is even considered highly desirable management experience. This forgiving attitude is what makes the technology sector so dynamic. A failure is rarely a dead end; it's just another opportunity. The unemployment rate in Silicon Valley—consistently lower than the national average—reflects this entrepreneurial spirit. Currently just 3 percent of Silicon Valley residents are jobless, versus 5.3 percent nationally.—*Forbes*, "Bouncing Back" (July, 1997)

Success exploits the seeds that failure plants. Failure contains tremendous growth energy.

Human efforts that fail dramatize the nobility of inspired, persistent human endeavor. Great achievements have been built on foundations of inadequacy and error. The discovery of America was made when Christopher Columbus took a wrong turn en route (he thought) to the East Indies. Charles Goodyear bungled an experiment and discovered vulcanized rubber. Sir Isaac Newton failed geometry, and Albert Einstein lacked an aptitude for math. Paul Gauguin was a failed stockbroker, and Alfred Butts invented the game of Scrabble® after he lost his job as an architect during the Depression. Robert Redford wanted to be a painter.

If failing can be seen as a necessary prelude to impressive achievement, then the process of succeeding itself can be better understood.

The aspiration and determination of an athlete to succeed when his body is ruined, of an engineer to build again when his bridge falls down, of a nation to prosper after its economy has crashed, or of a scientist to conduct years of unsuccessful experiments help us understand the origins of success. Their failures—sometimes quiet and interminable, sometimes quick and spectacular—define the foundations of success, and the spirit it needs.

While thinking about how I was taught values, I realized I was taught to value the effort and the exploration that came before success. I have found that failure and the analysis of failure have always been more interesting to me, and I learn something from them. I don't learn anything by basking in success. When I can honestly say, "I don't know," I begin to know. "I think of information as the oil in a piece of machinery," said Nathan Felde, the founding partner of Mezza. The information permits operation. There are a lot of systems now that are being designed by people who fail to notice that the exhaust pipe runs back into the passenger compartment. They are running along at quite a clip pouring exhaust into the cockpit or the passenger compartment; people are used to it; they have adjusted to a very high level of exhaust.

You Won't Believe What Went Wrong

> Flying is learning to throw yourself at the ground
> and miss.—Douglas Adams

In order to get to the bottom, in order to find what is there, you really do have to fail. We have a culture that sustains only the manifestation of success.

While many people probably aren't consciously aware of it, we all possess the capacity for endowing failure with more nobility—or at least with more humor and affections. When we look back on our lives, sometimes the things that we remember most fondly are the times when everything went wrong. I know a woman who could write a book about the terrible things that have happened to her on first days: the first day of school, the first day of a new job. Once she wore two different kinds of shoes and didn't discover it until the day was over. Another time she was beset by a case of static cling. After performing in what she thought was an exemplary manner during her first four hours at a new job, a co-worker informed her that she had a pair of rainbow-colored panties clinging to the back of her white blouse.

When people talk about their vacations, invariably what they recount with the most delight are the misadventures. Long after they have forgotten the names of the cathedrals and museums, they will remember the time they went to California and their luggage went to Caracas, when the hotel in Hong Kong lost their reservations and they spent the night in the hotel sauna, when they rushed to the JFK airport in New York to catch a plane that left from La Guardia.

Every exit is an entry somewhere else.—Tom Stoppard

In all my travels, one of my fondest memories was getting stuck on a hot runway in Jodhpur, India. I was en route to Jaipur, and the plane had mechanical difficulties. Airport personnel told us that we would be there for seven hours and would have to wait on the plane. I was the only foreigner on the plane. After an hour, I started berating the airline personnel. I insisted that they find a bus and take us into town so at least we could see the place and have lunch. They did. After letting everyone else off the bus at a restaurant, the driver turned to me and said, "You stay on the bus. You're going to get a tour of Jodhpur." We returned to the restaurant to find everyone else still waiting for lunch. Someone from the airlines came and, glaring directly at me, made an announcement, "The plane is ready now, but you are going to eat first."

We all happily recount our misadventures when it comes to travel. We should be able to do more of this in our professional lives. When John Naisbitt was questioned for acting as a business consultant after his own company almost went bankrupt, he asserted that for this very reason, he was a better consultant. He understood from experience what could go wrong in a company.

In my company, I respect the person who can come to me and say, "I'm sorry. I tried something, and it didn't work." I know that the person had learned something.

The Breaking Point

I am interested in failure because that is the moment of learning—the moment of jeopardy that is both interesting and enlightening. The fundamental means of teaching a course in structural engineering is to show the moment when a piece of wood breaks, when a piece of steel bends, when a piece of stone or concrete collapses. You learn by watching something fail to work. William Lear, who invented the jet that bears his name, invented a steam car and all sorts of other things that he was certain would fail. He felt that there was a cyclical relationship between failure and success, and that failure was the necessary first part of the cycle.

> Because a fellow has failed once or twice, or a
> dozen times, you don't want to set him down as
> a failure till he's dead or loses his courage—and
> that's the same thing.—George Lorimer

I often think one's life is molded more by inability than ability. When I visited the aerospace museum in Washington, D.C., as marvelous as it is, I missed the epiphany of things that failed. A few years ago, to celebrate the anniversary of the Wright airplane, there was an article in Scientific American about the Wright brothers and their inventions. It made me think about the beginning of that wonderful film, *Those Magnificent Men in Their Flying Machines*, in which you see a litany of failed aircraft. You laugh, but you also see how seriously involved everybody was in trying to fly. All the failure, all the things that didn't work, make you realize that the Wright brothers were really something. All the paths taken, all the good intentions, the logistics, the absurdities, all the hopes of people trying to fly testifying to the power we have when we refuse to quit.

Museum of Failure Is Overnight Success

There should be a museum dedicated to human inventive failure. The only problem it would face would be its overnight success. In almost any scientific field, it would add enormously to the understanding of what does work by showing what doesn't work. In developing the polio vaccine, Jonas Salk spent 98 percent of his time documenting the things that didn't work until he found the thing that did.

A scientist's notebook is basically a journal of negative results. Scientists try to disprove their ideas—that is the work they do. "Images become useful to scientists to the extent that they contain information that contradicts conventional wisdom, forming the basis of a polemical understanding of nature," according to Chandra Mukerji in a paper, "Imaginary Dialogues: The Practice of Picture-Making in Scientific Research," delivered at the International Sociological Association and published in 1986.

As economist Kenneth Boulding said, "The moral of evolution is that nothing fails like success because successful adaptation leads to the loss of adaptability…This is why a purely technical education can be disastrous. It trains people only in thinking of things that have been thought of and this will eventually lead to disaster."

If you put a camera on the Golden Gate Bridge and photographed it for twenty years, you wouldn't learn very much because the bridge succeeded. You learn much more from the documentation of failure. So failure can be defined as delayed success.

The anxiety associated with failure inhibits us from exploiting our creativity, from taking the risks that might lead us into new territory, and from learning and thus assimilating new information.

An acceptance of failure as a necessary prelude to success is imperative to reducing anxiety.

Some of My Failures

For most of my career, I was not successful. I couldn't glue two nickels together. At best, I kind of failed sideways my whole life, although to call some of what happened "sideways" would be to give it a pretty face.

> Apparent failure may hold in its rough shell the germs of a success that will blossom in time, and bear fruit throughout eternity.—Frances Watkins Harper

I started an architecture firm with two partners, and for thirteen years the firm never made it. My partners couldn't get clients, and I couldn't bear the idea of doing what some body said to do; I was kind of an angry young man. Before the firm could go bankrupt, we closed it. I had no idea what I was going to do. That was not a trivial failure. I mean, thirteen years of struggling is not a trivial amount of time. I've had lots of other failures.

Through the 1970s I lived thinly, although other people always thought I was rich, even when I was living in a third-floor garret over a restaurant kitchen in a bad part of Philadelphia and didn't own a car. People thought I was independently wealthy because I dressed badly and didn't care what I said at meetings. "You always must have had money," they'll say to me now. "I mean, you always did what you wanted to do." Yeah, and that's equated with money.

It was the only way people could explain it to themselves. By 1981, all I owned was a used Honda. I didn't have a business.

Despite my subsequent success with Access Press, the Smart Yellow Pages, then with Information Anxiety, and the TED conferences as they found an audience, I have continued with failures. I have a phrase, like a mantra, that I tell people all the time: "Most things don't work." This doesn't just refer to bad ideas. I have lots of ideas; more than that, I have lots of good ideas. Lots of my good ideas never happen for various reasons.

Wrong Is the New Right

By Nick Currie

I'm talking to a magazine editor. "You've got to do a thing about how wrong is the new right," I tell him. "Because if we don't give ourselves the right to get things wrong, there's no way we'll get anything right. We'll just repeat the way things were once right, but aren't any longer."

He likes the idea. "Can you call me Monday?" he says.

*

I'm talking to John Coltrane. Correction: I'm on hold, waiting for John Coltrane's people to put him on the line. I want to read back to him this great line I've heard he said: "There's no such thing as an error, it's only the next great new idea coming through." I want to ask him some questions about that.

"Mr. Coltrane, have you awarded yourself the right to be wrong? Mr. Coltrane, how do you increase the chance of accidents at work? Mr. Coltrane, if you could go back in time and make one great mistake you failed to make at the time, what would it be?" But I'm stuck on hold, with this very un-Coltrane-like classical muzak playing.

Eventually someone comes on and says "Can you call back Monday?"

(Later I discover that John Coltrane died in 1967. Shit!)

*

I'm speaking to magnificent zany old hippy Daevid Allen, who came to Paris from Australia in the sixties, steeped himself in Pataphysics, then founded Gong, the "flying teapot" band whose records were all set on the Planet Gong. At least I think I'm speaking to Daevid. The line is pretty hazy. Maybe the telephone got plugged right into Gaia; maybe I'm hearing the Invisible Opera Company of Tibet tuning up the spheres. It's pretty trippy, man.

When the line clears up I'll be asking Daevid why he named his new band University of Errors. Is he suggesting that errors teach us more than getting things right? Is this a reference to the College of Pataphysics? Does Daevid have a degree in Advanced Wrongness?

Eventually, through the cosmic jive, I hear a voice. "Can you call back Monday?" it asks.

*

So I've looked up the College of Pataphysics in the Yellow Pages. I'm quite surprised it's in there. They even have a quarter-page display ad. Under the heading "College of Pataphysics (established 1949)" it reads:

"Pataphysics, according to its founder Alfred Jarry (1873–1907), is the science of imaginary solutions. Pataphysics is by its very nature the science of the indefinable, the science of exceptions, anomalies, and the particular."

Then there's a list of famous graduates: Raymond Queneau, Julio Cortazar, Marcel Duchamp, and the Marx brothers. Excited, I dial the number. Put me down for a three-semester course in Advanced Anomaly! But there's just a recording. "Don't be the victim of a terrible seaweed accident," it says. "Leave your message after the tone."

I decide to call back Monday.

*

I'm trying to get through to the Mistakers. These guys I knew in New York back in 2000. A kind of art gang. Harmony Korine, Brian Degraw, Little Ricky who did T-shirts, Thuy, and Miho from preppy clothes label United Bamboo. They all had these devil's fork tattoos on their hands. They signed up to some kind of Mistaker Manifesto that committed them to making as many mistakes as possible in the shortest possible time. Harmony even started a film called "Fighting Harm," which was just him going into bars and insulting guys bigger than him until they started punching him. It was such a big and good mistake that he got badly hurt and abandoned the film.

Must've dialed the wrong number. Some guy going "Lotus Cafe, take your order?"

*

I'm speaking to Charles Thomson at Stuckism International, an art gallery on Charlotte Road in London's East End. I'm framing a few questions about the *Stuckist Manifesto* he wrote with Billy Childish in 1999. Did they really get their name when Tracey Emin—the art slag from Margate—shouted at Billy Childish—the goatee geezer out of Thee Headcoatees—that he was "stuck, stuck, stuck" in his work? And did Childish really turn that taunt into a virtue of some kind when he started Stuckism? Does the Stuckist really, as the manifesto says, understand "the futility of all striving"?

Is the Stuckist, unlike the successful professional conceptual artist with his "dead sheep and found underpants" (ooh, bitch!) really "unencumbered by the need to be seen as infallible" and "not afraid to fail"? Is the Stuckist really an amateur whose duty is "to always be wrong"?

Charles says those are pretty valid and relevant questions, and he'll get back to me on Monday.

*

I'm not having much phone luck today, so I go out and walk around downtown Berlin. So, vibe! Who should I bump into but Ali Smith, the Scottish novelist? We sit down at a street table and I ask her some questions.

Ali, do you try to engender accidents in your work? Do you try to change your habits to make what you're writing seem "wrong" to you? 'Cos I'm writing this article, and I've got a big investment in wrong being the new right.

Ali Smith: I am fascinated by accidents and the relationship of meaning to accident. The relationship of what seems like chance to what seems like meaning. That sense of the random, which is of course never random, because that's how our lives are made up, because they make narrative backwards. But if they made narrative first—which of course would always feel wrong, because how could you tell that it was narrative?—then maybe we would change our ways of understanding things.

Me: I'm confused. What do you mean, if we made narrative first?

Ali Smith: Okay, here we are, I met you, we're sitting in this street, some people are walking past, there's a narrative, there are several narratives going on. If we could be aware of all the narratives that are going on rather than the one we think is "the right narrative," then anything could happen; any shapes could happen; any story could happen.

*

Maybe it's the thirty-year-old Laphroaig whiskey we've been downing, but I'm suddenly quite excited by this idea of following all the little "wrong" narratives rather than the one big "right" one. Maybe I'll do that in my piece! It's drift, isn't it? It's what the Situationists called "derive"! You can do that on the street; you just follow your nose until you're in a gloomy area with a bunch of cranes and some seagulls and a greasy cafe. But who cares that it's a dank nowhere; you got here thanks to "derive" and "psychogeography," and that makes it fashionable.

Paging Guy Debord, dead Frenchman, Situationist, father of psychogeography, grandfather of punk marketing! White courtesy telephone, please.

*

So I'm drifting through the city, and I stumble across an art opening. It's a Christine Hill show called "Style Manual." Christine has illustrated a bunch of her prejudices on bits of paper, pages from a ring binder, and hung them on the wall. As you look at them, it becomes clear that she's making her own personal style manual, like the ones they have at corporations like the *New York Times* or UPS. Style manuals are books (or "bibles") containing rules, which, to employees, become a kind of corporate Ten Commandments. Thou shalt always use purple and orange Futura on a gray ground. Thou shalt never answer the phone without repeating the company slogan.

Christine Hill is there in person. She's smiling a lot, and she's hot. I figure she'll have some interesting things to say because this style manual thing is all about etiquette. It's about designating a whole bunch of things "right" and a whole other bunch of things "wrong." I flick on my tape recorder and approach.

Me: Christine, I'm interested in this style manual idea, and also this very retro style you're using. Is there some nostalgia for a time when everybody knew what was wrong and what was right?

Christine Hill: For me, definitely. I definitely feel nostalgia. It's not like trying to stay in one place but some things, especially visually, once they get to a certain point of design I wish they would stop being improved. Like the UPS logo—it was great, it didn't need improving. Corporate logos keep getting rounder and rounder. For me it was always helpful to know what is okay, what is not, and have it all kind of noted in a style manual.

Me: But things get right and then they're so right they're dead. And you have to tear up the style manual and start again. But you're not tearing up the style manual...

Christine Hill: Well, first I have to write it! But I get to write it, so that's the whole thing. I'm not tearing up the one that has been given to me. I'm getting to decide what it is.

Me: But you're agreeing with a lot of real people out there who have their own style manuals, like the *New York Times* style manual, which I see over there.

Christine Hill (getting gossipy): I've heard some great things about the Abercrombie & Fitch style manual. It's supposedly so top secret that I would almost have to go get a job there just to read what that thing is.

We talk for a while about why the FedEx logo is so vile, then I take her photo and drift out of the room.

*

So I'm stalking Klaus Biesenbach, the guy who curates all the best art shows I see at PS1, the ICA, Kunst-Werke—my favourite galleries in (darling!) New York, London, and Berlin. I want to ask him about a piece he chose for Video Acts, the single-channel 1970s video art show I just saw in London. In it, Vito Acconci is sitting at a table talking to the camera. "I need to imagine you're touching my cock; I need to imagine your hands are exploring my crotch and caressing my balls," he's saying. It's embarrassing to watch, because you just see this guy and imagine him wanking under the table while he's describing "you" doing all that stuff to him. But then again, the rawness and wrongness of that makes Acconci seem very vulnerable. And his need for "you" to watch him and feel his shame and see him belittled makes you like him.

Klaus isn't vulnerable. He's busy. Hedi Slimane is doing a book launch. "Why don't you call my office on Monday?" he says.

*

I'm Skyping with Scanner, the "artist who listens to the world then plays it back." Scanner is one of those smart laptop guys with a big shaved dome head that bobs around behind a Powerbook. He's probably read Kim Cascone's essay "The Aesthetics of Failure," which says that glitch is a form of music based on amplifying rather than minimizing mistakes. He probably knows that John Cage said that noise inevitably turns into harmony if you repeat it enough (and with recording technology, you can).

So I'm asking Scanner about being wrong.

Me: Has something you've created struck others—because of its sheer originality —as "wrong" when they first saw it?

Scanner: Morally wrong for certain. Early recordings of scanned phone calls were deemed outrageous and intruding on private space, especially by journalists writing for tabloids. Now media entertainment is saturated by a desire to endlessly watch and listen to others.

Me: Tell me about a happy accident or deliberate error that made you stronger or broke you through an impasse.

Scanner: I lost an entire album through a horrific system crash in my computer only to discover that the remnants offered something completely new, corrupted, distorted, and potentially useless that I later went on to exploit at length.

Me: If you could go back in time and make one mistake you failed to make when you had the chance, what would it be?

Scanner: I wish I'd known that scratching a record could be profitable. All those years of carefully handling vinyl and gently nudging the stylus across. Goodness, I really missed out there!

Me: Which artist or creator made your favorite mistake, and what is it?

Scanner: Andy Kaufman, the late American comedian, made the mistake of inviting his entire audience to a warehouse to offer them milk and cookies, only to discover afterwards that it cost more than the financial rewards of the show itself.

*

I've listened to Scanner, and I'm playing him back. That Andy Kaufman thing reminds me of two of my favorite mistakes. Both made by New Order on their Blue Monday.

One, Peter Saville's dye-cut lozenge sleeve cost so much

to manufacture that Factory Records actually lost two pence for every copy of the record they sold. A total marketing mistake. But a great sleeve. And two, that funky bit where the drum machine stops, rears up, shows the whites of its eyes, whinnies, and does this completely irrelevant kick drum part. Stephen Morris said that was totally a mistake because they'd just bought the drum machine and didn't know how to program it yet. But they liked it and decided to leave it in. Then a bunch of other bands copied the mistake, because it was the best thing in the record. Then the mistake became a new orthodoxy and you had to have it in your Electroclash record or be a folk singer. The wrong became so much the new right that it came full circle and went back to being wrong again.

Now the thing to be is a folk singer.

*

"Panthers broke into the temple," wrote Franz Kafka, "and drank the holy wine. They did the same thing the following year, and so on. Eventually it was incorporated into the ceremony."

At that point I guess a self-respecting panther would do something a bit more fresh, like helping old ladies cross the street.

*

I'm talking to Igor Stravinsky. He's calling me (collect) on a really bad line, from 1913. He's furious that a crowd of Parisians has just greeted his new work "The Rite of Spring" with boos and whistles. I ask him to call back on Monday. This call is costing me a bomb.

*

Apparently Wassily Kandinsky called while I was out. His message is a bit garbled, but it seems to be about how he came into his studio one day and saw a landscape he'd done propped on its

side, failed to recognize it, and saw instead this incredible impro-
visation made of pure color and form. The message ends "... and
that's how I invented abstract art. By accident! Put that in your
article!"

*

I call my mom and ask her if I was planned or a mistake.
And if I was a mistake, does that make me any less valid, you know,
as a person?

"I'm busy right now," says my mom. "Can you call back on
Monday?"

Memory,
Failure,
Imagin

By Peter Blegvad

and
tion

This experiment is part of the Imagined, Observed, Remembered project begun in 1976, an attempt to shed light on the murky world of interior vision. By "murky," I mean subjective. The project is an attempt to objectify subjective phenomena, to find languages, visual and verbal, to describe them.

Is inner vision transparent to itself? Will mental imagery submit to interview? Investigation of these questions is hampered by a kind of uncertainty principle: as Sartre says,[1] we can't verify the mental image at the same time as we're producing it. But, maybe because it's "impossible" and doomed to failure, that the challenge is irresistible.

While we don't receive mental images through the retina, it's not purely metaphorical to say that we "see" pictures in the mind's eye. Mental imagery is processed by the same part of the brain that deals with vision. As long as your visual cortex is intact, you'll have mental imagery, even if you were born blind. Asleep, with our eyes wide shut, in pitch darkness, we dream images that likewise bloom in the visual cortex.

Artists work from memory and imagination as readily as from observation. The following experiment is, first of all, an attempt to observe the image of an object REMEMBERED over time, as my memory of it fails, to document the process of this failure. But it's also intended to be a practical demonstration of the symbiosis between FORGETTING and IMAGINING. Memory merely "recognizes" an object, but imagination leads us further, to a "vision" of the thing. Imaginative vision involves a failure of memory in that we can't really see anew until we forget what we know.

The experiment has four stages:

1. The object is OBSERVED. A drawing is made "from life" (or, in this case, from a photograph) to imprint it on the memory. Object and drawing are then concealed from view.

2. Time passes.

3. The object REMEMBERED is depicted at intervals. A record of drift and attrition.

4. Over sufficient time, with sufficient drift, the object gradually becomes more IMAGINED than REMEMBERED. Does the resultant distortion constitute an imaginative vision of the object? I hope to demonstrate that it does.

In everyday life, the perceptual and conceptual functions of the mind work in concert to create a coherent picture of the world from fragments of data. This process is automatic, unconscious. Therefore, in order to depict a failure of memory with any degree of accuracy, one must first learn to disable or distract the conceptual function. Only then is one able to "see," in the mind's eye, the lacunary image of the thing imperfectly recalled, in fragments, without its being unified, filled in and "airbrushed" (idealized) to fit a conceptual model.

Unnatural effort and vigilance is required because memory, as Nietzsche said of the eye, "...finds it more comfortable to respond to a given stimulus by reproducing once more an image that it has produced many times before, instead of registering what is different and new in an impression." One has to override this natural tendency toward economy of effort in order to register the differences and novelties in a memory as it evolves over time.

From a practical point of view, the degree to which a memory departs from its source is seen, understandably, as "loss" or "failure"; but from a creative standpoint, a memory can be thought of as evolving, undergoing metamorphosis, until, like a word in a game of Chinese whispers, it is more IMAGINED than REMEMBERED, at which point it has become an independent image, autonomous, no longer a record or reflection of something else.

Drawing a Lion from Memory

First, before exposing myself to the image of a caged lion, I tried to draw one as realistically as I could. A record of the "innocence" I was about to lose.

Fig. 1

Working from this photograph, found in an old encyclopaedia, ...

Fig. 2

... I drew this image of a recumbent lion.

Fig. 3

Fig. 1

Fig. 4

Fig. 2

Fig. 5

Fig. 3

Six months later, I tried to recreate it from memory.

Fig. 4

I aborted this first attempt when I realized that, whenever I experienced a failure of recall, as I frequently did, the missing detail would be filled in automatically by other memories in the constellation of knowledge of which my memory of the lion observed (Figs. 1 and 2) was a part.[2] Whatever attrition and drift the image might have sustained over the past six months, it was hidden under bits of other lions (felines in general) remembered.

Fig. 5

In my second attempt, therefore, I concentrated on isolating the specific image I wanted: my memory of the lion observed. Unless I could "see" a detail in my mind's eye, I left it out or indicated its absence with crosshatching, a "cloud of unknowing."

Ears, nose, mouth, hind legs have all drifted off, but the sphinx-like creature with front paw extended in Fig. 5 is still recognizably a reflection of the lion observed. The bars of the cage with patches of foliage behind have also proved to be adhesive.

Fig. 6

Two years later, the details have dissolved, leaving only a vague impression of hindquarters, front paw, mane, and the distinctive head, like the outline of a skull. These stand out in white against a night of amnesia. The bars of the cage remain, although their terminal points are lost. The image required a more impressionistic rendering, in pencil and wash. Despite or perhaps because of its economy, the result is a surprisingly "legible" sign for lion.

However, the beast now points with its paw to the right. I've long been haunted by incipient dyslexia. Reversed orientation is a common failure of memory.[3]

Fig. 7

This curious variant was produced a few days after drawing Fig. 6. Here the ambiguity of orientation expresses itself in a doubling or mirroring of the few details—head, mane, and extended paw—that I remembered most vividly. Brightness is again used to indicate clarity of recall, but the mane is now luminous, an aura, evidence that imagination is now participating to a greater extent in the creation of the image.

Fig. 8

Experts agree; every act of imagination involves a degree of amnesia. As senility encroaches and memory fails, I console myself with Blake: "Imagination has nothing to do with Memory"; with Nietzsche: "In order to create, it's necessary to forget"; and with Paul Valéry: "To see something truly is to forget its name."

Fifteen months since drawing the double lion in Fig. 7. By now, enough has been forgotten for imagination to seize the reins from memory. In Fig. 8, the bars are gone, although the lion is by no means "free." The image is still the product of constraining influences from a constellation of sources. What's different is that imagination has combined these to produce a drawing that makes us look twice. In the first of these two looks, before we recognize, we see.

As William James points out, "the taste for emotions of recognition" (based on remembering) is countered or accompanied

Fig. 6

Fig. 9

Fig. 10

Fig. 7

Fig. 11

Fig. 8

Fig. 12

Fig. 13

by "the taste for emotions of surprise" (based on forgetting/imagining). Amnesia is selective. Discovery of the often unconscious criteria by which we select certain memories to suppress while sparing others is usually the province of psychoanalysis, but the practice of art also brings these occult processes to light. Consider Pessoa: "My vision of things always suppresses in them that which my dreams cannot use.... Sometimes the best way to see an object is to annihilate it, but it still subsists, how I have no idea, made out of the very matter of its negation and abolition ..."[4] It seems to me that the forgetting involved in the production of the lion in Fig. 8 was, at least on one level, an editing ("annihilating") process with a criteria not dissimilar to Pessoa's.

The lion's head or face is involved in a constellation of its own.

Fig. 9 (detail of Fig. 8)

Its form is influenced by, among other things, an Amerindian glyph from a book of symbols, ...

Fig. 10

... by images of skulls and radiant suns like these, ...

Figs. 11 and 12

... and, unexpectedly, by a drawing of "pants on fire" illustrating a review of a book about lying,[5] which I recently drew for the *New York Times*.

Fig. 13

Endnotes

1. Sartre, *The Psychology of Imagination*, "We cannot study the image we are 'seeing' in the mind, because to do so would demand that at a given moment we should be able to stop producing [the image], in order to verify the result.... This cannot happen in imaginative consciousness."
2. A constellation of associations evoked by "lion" would include: mane, loin, lino, sun, fire, pride, gold, courage, king, roar, blood, meat—images ranging from heraldry to Bert Lahr in *The Wizard of Oz*.
3. Like a mirror, memory reverses right and left but not up and down.
4. *The Book of Disquiet.*
5. Lyin' = lion?

Overcommitment: A Recipe for Failure

By Ina Saltz

The word looms large. It hangs over one's head. The fear of it is a whip to spur one on ... faster, more, further, lest one topple into the abyss of ... F A I L U R E .

Our ever-quickening culture of expectations, responsibilities, obligations, commitments ... piling up into huge heaps, a never-ending, impossible-to-conquer, Sisyphean task or, as a friend once described it, "the daily battle of loose ends."

How can anyone truly feel successful when success itself typically generates even more expectation of success? Perhaps the key to a successful life lies in having low expectations (that's always been my key to "success" in golf), but in real life, isn't it desirable to be as productive, as connected, as active as possible? To be "firing on all pistons"? Isn't that why we were put here on earth?

If accomplishments define your self-worth, then it is inherently worthy to strive ... but how to know when you've over-reached?

By failing, of course. And that is where life's lessons really kick in.

I have always taken certain competencies for granted. So, when little things start to go wrong, it suddenly seems as if everything is built on a house of cards, where one card slips and things quickly escalate into a chain reaction of missed cues, missed deadlines, missed appointments.

Failure for me is the ever-lurking by-product of overcommitment, especially commitments undertaken with the best of intentions. True, I am particularly driven (people assume I must have a few clones toiling away for me in some dark closet). But how can we determine when we have reached our limit if not by, on occasion, exceeding our limitations? This has been the all-consuming question of my life.

Here are some of the things that start to happen when I am particularly stressed by a lengthening "to-do" list: forgetting my watch (okay, I can still check the time on my cell phone, but still, it's a sign that all is not well); forgetting my school keys and ID ("I'm locked out; can you call security? Honest, I really am a faculty member here"); forgetting which class I am teaching ("but, Professor Saltz, this is Type 2! That wasn't our homework assignment!"); forgetting a lunch or some other appointment (cell phone rings: "Where are you?!"); or showing up at the wrong place (cell phone rings: "Where are you?!"); or, worst of all, leaving my little purse on the bus (keys, cash, photos, makeup, Metrocard ... all sadly never recovered) or my tennis racquet in a cab (a good excuse to buy a new racquet). Last week, I forgot my shirt for my weekly game of doubles, so I played in my sports bra (no one really noticed).

These "little" failures are warning signs, warnings to alert me to the impending larger failures of unfulfilled promises, unmet commitments, public humiliation. "Get a grip!" they warn. "Be realistic; you've already bitten off more than you can chew ... alert! Alert!"

I have come to recognize these little failures as the warning signs they are, and generally I take heed ... although that continues to be a challenge for me. Whirling constantly in my head is a mental rolodex of shoulds and musts … couple that with a predisposition to want to please, to avoid saying "no" … and the fear that if I do, no one will ask again. (Yes, I know; a good therapist could really help with those last couple of items. I'm working on it … really.)

Always, there seem to be too many things on my plate … and this represents another kind of FAILURE … an inability to properly judge what I can accomplish in an allotted time, combined with a tireless optimism that somehow I can do it all. In my younger days that meant skating at Roxy until 1 or 2 AM every night, doing freelance work at home for a couple of hours, then tumbling into bed for a few hours of sleep and somehow getting to work the next day by 10 AM youthful stamina can counterbalance perpetual sleep deprivation, but those days are long gone.

I've racked up a pretty impressive résumé by now. Of course, the by-product of all those accomplishments is the admiration of others (little do they know about all those small disasters) and the inevitable requests that follow.

If you want something done, the saying goes, ask a busy person.

Next time, please … give us busy people a break. We're only human.

When Things Go Wrong

By Amanda Bowers

Things go wrong. For the designer, the creative process often falls victim to accident, and things don't always go as planned. For some, the unexpected or the threat of failure looms as a constant threat and becomes something we try to avoid. But instead of fearing the unknown in this way or turning it into a kind of designer anxiety, the accidental has many qualities that could be embraced.

How do we cope with the unknown and possibility of failure? Expectation and past experience deeply influence our behavior in the face of uncertainty. The Bayesian approach is to provide a mathematical basis for the re-examination of one's existing beliefs in the light of new evidence. In other words, it allows scientists to combine new data with their existing knowledge or expertise. People have been using Bayesian analysis in everyday life long before the method was formalized. When crossing the street, pedestrians rely both on what they see and what they remember about the speed of cars on similar roads. The canonical example is a child observing its first sunset, wondering whether the sun will rise again or not.[1] As the sun rises each morning, the child becomes more and more confident in the event's occurrence until its occurrence is no longer a question.

According to a recently published study surrounding Bayesian analysis, the more uncertainty that individuals face, the more likely they are to base decisions on their subconscious memory and the less on what they actually see. New research stands out because it highlights the tipping point at which uncertainty becomes great enough to give past experience more credibility than current observation. Looking to past experience provides a coping strategy for dealing with the unknown. But relying only on subconscious memory in the face of the unknown denies the opportunity to learn from or to use the unexpected.

Writer and theorist Paul Virilio pushes against this fear of the unknown. Inspired by the introduction of the chaos theory in the 1970s, Virilio asks that we make room for fallibility so that the idea of progress can be understood in a new way. He says, "The beginning of wisdom would be, above all, an awareness of symmetry between substance and accident…If we are to really understand progress as something other than linear and continuous, we must consider the beneficent error."

One of Virilio's chief goals is to familiarize researchers, scientists, and engineers, among others, with the idea of the unexpected so that they might better avoid the dangers of routine. He asserts that "Habit is a 'deformity' that comes from a complacent belief that technology works flawlessly." As operations become increasingly automatic, consciousness exists only for accidents. But technology, particularly with mass production, does have a tendency to malfunction or to fail to perform in the manner expected. How can technology be re-evaluated in the face of such failure? Virilio uses the invention of the train as an example: To invent the train was to also invent its derailment. Without the error of the derailment, there would be no train. He says that there is "no gain without a corresponding loss. If to invent the substance is, indirectly, to invent the accident, then the more powerful and efficient the invention, the more dramatic the accident."

Just about everyone has shared the flush of anxiety at a computer's error message or has been puzzled by the mysterious transformation that occurred somewhere between a computer screen and a printer's output. In my explorations, I have tampered with unstable technologies, transposed fallible human qualities onto machines, and borrowed from the visual language of errors, glitches, and hiccups. What does this reveal about the technology? Or about the process and the intended versus actual outcome? Or even about the user of the technology?

By its very definition, the accident cannot be contrived, but some of its behaviors and their consequences can be incorporated into the creative process. I have found embracing the accidental or unexpected to be a more generative way of working. For example, using a system that cannot be completely controlled is one way of allowing unpredictable elements into the work. Even aspects of inevitability and predictability can be used against moments of chance behavior in a way that allows for new and unexpected outcomes in the design process. My desire to work with this phenomenon has led me to question the role of the designer as an orchestrator and to find a usable definition of the accident. How can the designer work with the accidental if he or she cannot control it? How does the designer incorporate failures into his or her process?

Does the accident have the power to illuminate or imply meaning? According to Aristotle, the accident reveals the substance of a thing. Virilio asserts that the accidental happening acts as a kind of analysis of what lies beneath knowledge and progress. For example, a Freudian slip is considered a verbal mistake that is thought to reveal an unconscious belief, thought, or emotion. This mistake has a consequence that is thought to be more truthful because of its lack of intention. How can this play out across design? The ability to determine intentionality often lies in the visibility of process. If a viewer is able to see evidence of what preceded an error, glitch, or hiccup, that abnormality is read. This reveals a sort of imbedded narrative that takes the viewer through the act of the mistake and to a new level of understanding. My ultimate goal is to move from the accident as subject to the unexpected as a lens through which the viewer gains another level of understanding.

Why is the accidental or erroneous so appealing? Perhaps because there is a certain human quality about them. The philosopher Odo Marquard suggests that the accidental is, in fact, what makes us human. In his essay, "In Defence of the Accidental," Marquard presses against an earlier philosophical idea that we are constructed through our choices and intentions. He asserts that we are, in fact, products of our accidents.

Endnote

[1] The Economist, September 30, 2000. The story continues: The child assigns equal prob-
abilities to both possible outcomes, and represents this by placing one white and one
black marble into a bag. The following day, when the sun rises, the child places another
white marble in the bag. The probability that a marble picked randomly from the bag will
be white (the child's degree of belief in future sunrises) has then moved from one half to
two-thirds. After sunrise the next day, the child adds yet another white marble, and the
probability increases from two-thirds to three-quarters. And so on. Gradually, the initial
belief that the sun is just as likely as not to rise each morning is modified to become a
near-certainty that the sun will always rise again.

f.

Succeeding om Failure

Nothing Succeeds like Failure: The Maverick Tendency in Graphic Design

By Ken Garland

Exactly two-hundred years ago the godfather of graphic designers produced an illuminated book of his own poems. Printed by
a unique method of relief etching on copper that he claimed had
been revealed to him in a vision by his late brother, each copy was
to be overpainted, usually in delicate watercolours but occasionally
in opaque pigments, including gold and silver. Originally thought
of as a children's book and intended, it seems, to be a steady earner
or even a runaway bestseller, it turned out to be something quite
other: a provocative, totally original collection of thoughts and images, not for children but about childhood and innocence.

The book was of course, *Songs of Innocence* and its creator
was William Blake, a 31-year-old engraver ten years out of his
apprenticeship and by that time reasonably well-established in his
craft. He had tried his hand with this method of printing about a
year before in a more modest work, *There is No Natural Religion*,

but with *Songs* he blossomed into an astonishing maturity in his confident handling of design and production.

We graphic designers may claim with pride that our trade, that is the effective fusion of words and images as an integrated and reproducible whole, began its revival with this splendid book. (Revival rather than birth, because Blake, consciously or unconsciously, was returning to the example of the illuminated mediaeval manuscript.) But a steady earner it was not, let alone a runaway bestseller. Each copy of the book was completed with the most meticulous and time-consuming care. Though Blake had at one time believed that he had devised "a method of printing both letterpress and engraving in a style more ornamental, uniform and grand, than any before discovered, while it produces works at less than one fourth of the expense,"[1] but this was not to be. As Bindman points out, "In practice, relief-etching in Blake's hands did not become a means of mass-reproduction…In fact Blake found himself expending the care of a mediaeval illuminator upon individual copies, finishing and colouring each one by hand. The Songs of innocence as Blake printed in became a rare and precious book."[2]

There are only just over twenty copies of the book in existence (Erdman[3] suggests 21, Bindman[4] 22 and Raine[5] 23), and there exist twenty-seven others in a combined grouping with the later *Songs of Experience* (1794). It is highly unlikely that Blake printed more than a hundred copies in total and possible that he did not print more than fifty or so. Each of the extant copies is a unique art work, no two copies having identical colouring.

If Songs was a commercial failure his later, larger format works were even more so. Of the dozen or so illuminated books he published between 1789 and 1820, none was any more successful, financially, than *Songs*. Of his last completed work, *Jerusalem*, the emanation of the giant Albion, consisting of a hundred intricately designed plates, he printed five copies and, as far as we know, only illuminated one. Even this one was unsold and when Blake died in 1827 it remained in the possession of his wife Catherine until her death in 1831.

How could such an enterprise have been pursued with such glorious zeal for so long and with so little reward?

Exactly a hundred years ago a 17-year-old art student was slung out of Royal Academician Hubert von Herkomer's school at Bushey, Herts, for fooling around in the life class. He took off for Paris and signed on at the Academie Julien, at that time the trendiest art school around. Despite the presence of fellow students Bonnard, Vuillard and Gauguin's enthusiastic disciple Serusier, Post-Impressionism appears to have passed him by completely: He was a Whistlerian when he arrived and a Whistlerian when he returned to England in 1890. However, he did bring back a deep admiration for the posters that were emblazoned on the streets of Paris, particularly those of Jules Cheret, whose joyful "Cherettes" pranced their way through 15 or more of the master's posters that were to be seen on the hoarding during his time there. It was borne in upon him that posters were not only a fit subject for an artist's interest: They were themselves an art form. He shared his enthusiasm with a friend and fellow artist, some five years older than himself. They kept a keen eye on the Parisian poster scene and were both bowled over by the first of Toulouse-Lautrec's posters—"Moulin Rouge: la Goulue" of 1891, then the "Reine de Joie," "Divan Japonais," and "Aristide Bruant" of 1892. The strong outlines, the flat areas of colour and the optical switch between convincing representation at one instant and two-dimensional abstraction at the next, were a revelation to them.

The older man was James Pryde and the younger was William Nicolson. When Nicholson married Pryde's sister Mabel, also an ex-student from Herkomer's (who had, by the way, also misbehaved herself in the life class by introducing a flock of geese into it one day[7]), her brother moved in to live with them. The two men, then 26 and 21, decided to emulate their French poster heroes. They were to become a design team under the name of J and W Beggarstaff; they would become rich and famous; the profits from one art form would thus finance the others. Quite a good plan, but it didn't work out.

For one thing, they were such rank amateurs. They really hadn't a clue. They began by submitting four designs entitled "Nobody's washing blue," "Nobody's candles," "Nobody's pianos," and "Nobody's nigger minstrels" to an exhibition of poster art at the Royal Aquarium, Westminster, in 1894. Their idea was that, having composed a few designs at whim, without a specific client in mind, they could then hawk them round town to the highest bidder, whose product name would then be superimposed on a space left for this purpose in the artwork. This was the case with their beautiful design "Girl reading," which they modified for the publishers Macmillan, retitled "The girl on the sofa." The client still didn't like it, and it was not produced.

For another thing, they had bad luck. Two posters commissioned by the actor-manager Henry Irving, though paid for, were never used because of the collapse of the theatrical productions they were to publicize.

The final blow to their plan was the philistine indifference of those who could have been their clients. As Nicholson's biographer, Lillian Browse, pointed out in 1956, "If only a small group of enlightened advertisers had taken advantage of the brilliance of these two young men's work, perhaps our hoardings today would not rank among the poorest it is possible to find…"[8] A rather harsh judgment of sixty years of British poster design but not entirely without justification. The truth is that only two of their posters— for Rowntree's Elect Cocoa and for *Harper's* magazine—had a widespread showing, and the latter was produced only after it had first been peddled around. As Pryde recalled, he and Nicholson thought the design, done on spec according to their plan, "particularly appropriate for a beef extract. We took it to the office of the firm in question and pinned it up on the wall of the very small room into which we were shown. After a while, the art editor or manager or whatever he called himself, a dear old gentleman rather like Father Christmas in appearance, came into the room; he gave the poster one glance and went out to of the room without saying anything. Later, it was offered to Sir George Alexander, who had a beefeater on the hoardings of the St. James's Theatre, but he did not find it suitable. Still later, that poster was redeemed by the proprietors of *Harper's* magazine, who reproduced it freely in the United States, and it also had a vogue here for the same purpose."[9]

Nicholson and Pryde abandoned their brief foray into poster design and pursued their separate careers, the former to his sturdy woodcuts and his safe portraiture, the latter to his stage acting and his stagey painting. Paradoxically this was the very moment at which their reputation was about to take off. The apotheosis of J and W Beggarstaff came about, not as a result of their display on hoardings, which was minimal, but through the pages of periodicals, most especially those that sprang up at the turn of the century to record and celebrate splendours of what they called "the Art of the Street." The most prominent and authoritative of these, Les Maîtres de L'Affiche, showed their *Harper's* poster in an issue of its 1896 volume, the unused poster for the ill-fated Don Quixote in 1897, and the Rowntree's Elect Cocoa poster in 1899. These seminal designs were to be reproduced again and again. By 1924 Walter Shaw Sparrow could claim, writing of the Don Quixote in his Advertising and Britsh Art, that "the great poster was reproduced for distribution in magazines, and its influence circulated throughout Europe… Today its merit is a highly valued example to most reformers."[10] In the same year E. McKnight Kauffer acknowledged a designer's grateful debt to the Beggarstaffs in his book *The Art of the Poster*. He was one of many, before and after this date, who were equally indebted, whether they acknowledged it or not.

How could such an apparently casual, patently uncommercial and sadly short-lived design practice have had such a profound influence on us graphic designers for nearly a hundred years?

Exactly fifty years ago a new-born baby confronted the East End of London as World War I moved into its third month. During the Blitz that followed he and his family were twice bombed out of their home; after the second occasion he was to spend two years in hospital. What effect this had on the mental health of the infant can only be guessed at, but fifty years later, he says, he is "still crawling out of the rubble."[13]

The baby, whose name is Ken Campbell, turned into a graphic designer and poet. Not all at once. The poetry started when he was about 14 or 15 but had to remain a closet activity because his mates would have ragged him rotten if they'd ever found out, and it didn't surface until some ten years later. Graphic design was his third career choice. First, he expressed a juvenile wish to become a doctor. His mother, thinking he had said he wanted to be a docker (which was her husband's trade) was aghast. So he went off, at age 16, to be an apprentice printer. Whilst doing day release at the London College of Printing, he was taught by Henry C. Beck, the creator of the London Underground Diagram. To his fellow apprentices, Beck appeared to have been stuck with them because no one else on the staff wanted the job, he was a bit of an old fusspot but to Campbell "there was only one word for his influence on me: pivotal."[12] Through Beck he discovered that there was a view of the visual handling of information that went far beyond the equivalent of cake-icing and fancy wrapping that passed (and still passes) for graphic design in some quarters.

He gave up his apprenticeship and became a full-time design student at the School. On leaving he embarked on the orthodox stage of his career—if you can call panic-driven paste up work at *Private Eye* magazine orthodox. (Campbell describes it as "a working class squit trapped in a box with a bunch of upper-class tossers.") Subsequent employment in established designers' studios was rather more congenial, but for someone as turbulent as he it was an experience he wished to move on from as soon as possible, so he took to freelance design and to teaching, first at Bristol, then at North East London Polytechnic, Bath Academy of Art, the Central School of Art and Design, Norwich School of Art and Brighton Polytechnic.

It was while he was at North East London Polytechnic that he wrote, designed and printed his first book, *A Few Ways Through the Window* in 1974-5, followed by *Terror Terror* in 1977. The next year he made Father's hook at Bath Academy of Art. With this he achieved a balance of strength and sensitivity that has been a hallmark of all his subsequent output.

In 1984 three books emerged from a fruitful fellowship year at Norwich School of Art of which one, *Broken Rules* and *Double Crosses* (verbal and visual punning is a vital feature of his work is a magnificent achievement—for me, the most powerful and moving he has yet produced. It exemplifies in the clearest way Campbell's methodical development of a single leitmotiv or idée fixe—in this case the pivoting of clumps of broken wooden letterpress rules about four fixed points—which is pursued obsessively, to the extent that it either turns you off or takes you over completely, so that you being to read into the variation a whole world of references: to the human body; to flying figures; to type characters; to semaphore signals; and eventually to the stark symmetry of the cross, when the brutal significance of the jagged fracture of the ends of the clumps becomes apparent. (The writer should here, perhaps, own up to his fondness for what is mistakenly but understandably called "minimalist" art, in which one phrase, or figure, or sound, is repeated with only barely perceptible variation. Accordingly, phone conversations between Campbell and the author always begin in this fashion: "Ken"; "Ken?"; "Ken!"; "Ken." A mundane interpretation of this exchange might ascribe it to Campbell's defective hearing, but both Kens know this is not so: They know that the word in Hebrew stands for Yes, and that they are genuinely engaged in an affirmative ritual.)

Campbell's books are produced in very limited editions—rarely more than fifty—and at a price per copy that is much higher than most people might think of paying for a mere book;

but it is important to note that they are not incursions by a "fine" artist into livres de peintres in the manner of those undertaken by such as Matisse and Bonnard for the publisher Vollard at the turn of the century. They are not showcases for art but integrated works by a poet-craftsman, thoroughly trained in typographic skills. They are undoubtedly the work of a maverick graphic designer who has turned away from orthodox client relationships because he has had, in his own words, "enough interfacing with Babylon"[13] yet continues to work in the mode of graphic design.

How comes it that such an apparently inappropriate use of skills that were devised for the service of commerce has produced works that can inspire designers and non-designers alike; that will, in the writer's estimation, come to be seen as a uniquely impressive fusion of words and images into an integrated and reproducible whole?

This question, and those similar questions arising from the work of Blake and the Beggarstaffs, can have only one answer: It is entirely feasible to produce work of the highest merit in graphic design that is independent of any client requirement or commission, independent of any perceived consumer need, and in the last resort independent of those so-called "laws" of supply and demand dear to the hearts of those who enthuse about the market economy. This independent spirit, so familiar in the field of fine art, literature or music, may appear incongruous in graphic design. Is there any place for mavericks in our trade or profession, or whatever it is, in the 1990s? Should we make room for them? Should we cherish them?

Maybe we should. God knows, there's enough money swilling about in the business to spare some of it for them; and God knows, we need them. We need, too, to be able to spot them before they drop out of sight from neglect, if we are to have the benefit of their innovation. It may flower only briefly, as it did with the Beggarstaffs, fading before we know it was there.

One thing is for sure: we need them more than they need us.

Paper given at Word and Image, Annual Conference of the Design History Society. City University, London, September 1989.

Endnotes

1. *Prospectus of 10*, October 1793, quoted by Bindman 1978, p14.
2. Bindman, David, *The Complete Graphic Works of William Blake*. London 1978, p.15.
3. Erdman, David V, *The Illuminated Blake*. London 1975, p.41.
4. Bindman, David, *Blake as an Artist*. Oxford 1977.
5. Raine, Kathleen, *William Blake*. London 1970, p.46.
6. Ibid, p.156.
7. Robinson, Duncan, *Introduction to Arts Council Catalog*. William Nicholson. London 1980, p.4.
8. Browse, Lillian, *William Nicholson*. London 1956, p.15.
9. Quoted in Hudson, Derek, James Pryde. London 1949, pp.25-6.
10. *Sparrow*, pp.71-2.
11. Conversation with the writer, 6 September 1989.
12. Ibid.
13. Ibid.

he Failure
f Success/
he Success
f Failure

By Warren Lehrer

A long long time ago, God dropped something (perhaps a cosmic thought), and it caused a very big bang, which set into motion a universe of never-ending accidents. According to experts, all matter and energy were knotted up into a supremely concentrated state, which burst into gazillions of pieces that continued to expand (although things have settled down quite a bit since that initial bang). Of course, experts have been wrong before. One divinely inspired theory had it that the universe was created in six days, and the earth was situated at its center. Even though this has been disproved, tens of millions of people still cling to this belief. Other experts were convinced that the earth was flat. To this day, people refer to the sun rising and setting on the basis of the failed flat earth model. We now know that the earth rotates on its axis every twenty-four hours, resulting in day and night, but we continue to refer to the sun rising and setting because it is a more comprehensible and thus more successful metaphor. Who can argue with all the successful songs, poems, movies, and boulevards inspired by the sun rising and setting? Failure does not preclude success. And vice versa.

Dinosaurs successfully roamed the earth for millions of years until (according to one prevalent theory) a piece of debris left over from the big bang crashed into the earth and caused a fire-storm and then an ice age. Such is life in a universe of (seemingly) random events. One day you're the head honcho; the next day you're a goner. This is also true of empires. They wage and win wars and gain control of more territory. They get to write the history for a while. Inevitably, they overreach and fail of their own hubris.

Our ancestors walked on all fours and lived naked in the wilderness. Over time, our brains enlarged, fingers distinguished themselves from toes, and we covered our private parts, figured out how to hunt, burrowed into caves, and drew pictures of our experiences on the walls of our homes. Eventually we figured out how to make clothes, how to farm, and how to build buildings, bridges, banks, bureaucracies, and bombs.

I was born on a hot summer day, mid-twentieth century. I had a slight heart murmur and scoliosis, but my parents (who were hoping for a girl) still considered me a minor miracle. Why they named me after a small hole in the ground that rodents live in, I'm not exactly sure. Even before I was born, my parents loved me the best way they knew how. My mother—a few months pregnant with me—followed her doctor's orders and took a "wonder drug" called Diethylstilbestrol (DES) every day for nearly seven months until I was born. DES is a synthetic form of estrogen that millions of pregnant women (from 1940-1971) took in order to prevent miscarriage and help produce a healthy, hefty baby. The drug was a great success for pharmaceutical companies (most prominently Eli Lilly), even though it turned out to be bad news for many of the female offspring who developed various forms of vaginal and cervical cancers. The male offspring has faired a little bit better, although we have higher incidences of testicular cancers and urinary disorders compared to men in the general population. I have a theory about another effect of this failed drug (although I am neither a doctor nor a scientist). Since millions of male fetuses were doused for months on end in huge quantities of female hormones, a certain percentage of male baby boomers have more feminine traits than any generation before or since. I like to think this had something to do with all the peace and social justice movements and the creative explosion that burst forth in the 1960s and that placed human values and imagination over domination and destruction. Then again, many people say that the ideals of that era have proved to be a failure. Who the hell knows what is failure and what is success? I offer no definitive answers here, only sweeping questions and a few personal memories.

When I was in college, I showed one of my painting professors some of my secret drawings that combined words and letterforms with images. He wagged his finger in my face and told me I was barking up the wrong tree. "Words and images are two different languages. They are not meant to coexist. Take my word for it, Warren, it's best to keep them separate." I left his office feeling like I had been given a mission in life. And for better or worse, I've been combining words and images ever since.

Another art professor in college encouraged my quirky experiments and turned me on to concrete poetry, the books of Dieter Roth, the assemblages of Kurt Schwitters, and the intricate typographic collages of Norman Ives. This professor, named Louie Finkelstein, told me I might be able to study with Norman Ives if I got into the graduate program at Yale in graphic design. I barely knew what graduate school was let alone graphic design, but I had heard of Yale. (I was a working class kid attending the City College of New York, which was tuition-free at the time.) Two years after my conversation with Louie Finkelstein, I was being interviewed by Norman Ives himself in a neo-gothic room in New Haven, Connecticut. He was looking at one of my fifty-foot-long painting scrolls. I had painted these scrolls on the floor of the bedroom/studio I rented. As free-spirited and impulsive as I was at the time, I always made sure to cover the floor with newspapers before painting away like a crazy person. Often when I primed my canvasses, the gesso would seep through the canvas and chunks of newspaper would attach itself to the back of the canvas. Norman Ives—who by this time was a fairly sick man—was looking at the gessoed-newspapered side of my painting scroll—not the side I had painted. His hands were shaking as he studied the scroll with the eye that didn't have a patch over it. Hesitantly, I told him that my painting, my art, was on the other side of the scroll, and he was looking at the side that was purely accidental. He looked at me with his good eye and a stern smile and said, "Don't put this down. You made this! And I think it's wonderful." I got into Yale, but Norman Ives died before I arrived, and I never got to study with him.

Speaking of failure and disease and how it can lead to success, there is the matter of synesthesia (which is not really a disease, although it sounds like one). One of my dictionaries defines synesthesia as a neurological condition that results in a confusion of the senses. Another dictionary defines it as a condition in which two or more bodily senses are coupled. It also provides etymology: from the Greek *syn-* meaning union and *aesthesis* meaning sensation. However you define it, synesthesia can result in hearing colors, tasting words, feeling the texture of numbers, etc. We are all born with this fluid interrelation of senses (hence ear, nose, and throat doctors). As we get older, we're schooled to separate our senses into compartments. Our synesthetic selves are systematically drummed out of us. Writing is separated from image-making, sounds from colors, imagination from reality, spirituality from science, fine arts from applied arts. To succeed as grown ups, we need to focus on areas of specialization. Depending on when and where we were born, to what gender, class, and race, and what opportunities we're exposed to, we may become street sweepers, homemakers, smelling experts, taste-testers, pistol-whippers, cold-cutters, meat-grinders, copywriters, or typographers. When I was in junior high school, I was herded into subterranean rooms to learn how to work with my hands. If I had turned out to be the girl my parents had hoped for, I would have taken typing and home economics. Since I was a boy, I took shop. Shopkeepers initiated us with stories of careless boys chopping off their hands in metal cutters, slicing off fingers on band saws, or electrocuting themselves into comas. Petrified by the prospect of losing limbs or consciousness, I was drawn to the letterpress shop, which required very little manual dexterity and felt more like playing with blocks. The print shop teacher taught me how to compose a text by using a composing stick, plucking one character at a time from a job case, letters formed words, words formed sentences, and sentences composed themselves into stories. By the time I was in college, I was an art major who wrote a lot on the side. I also played and composed music. I tried to keep it all separate, I swear. Alas, my attempts to follow the rules and compartmentalize were a failure.

Doomed never to fit into one discrete category, my work over the past twenty-seven years has found its way into the lunatic fringes of half a dozen different fields. I could take offense at still being called an experimentalist at the advanced age of half a century and ask the question: After how many decades and how many books and multimedia projects can it be said that I am no longer merely experimenting? Instead, I celebrate having no clear map to follow, other than the one I continue to draw and redraw for myself. Unlike Michelangelo, who was said to chip everything away from a block of stone that wasn't the artwork he envisioned perfectly in his head, I am a head banger. I grovel, scrape, scratch out, rip apart, put back together, cut, paste, work and re-work, then bang my head against the wall every which way until something begins to ooze out of the nothingness and surprises me. I plod along doggedly like this for two or three years until a work finishes itself. If it's a book, I send it off to the printer and wait to get the first bound copy. When it finally arrives, I'm usually deflated. While I'm working on the thing, it lives fluidly in the boundless realm of the imagination. Once the book is printed and captured between two covers, it becomes just one more finite object in the world, riddled with flaws, susceptible to mildew, floods, and misinterpretations. I hold the virgin book in my hands, open it expectantly, and begin reading. I see it objectively for the first time. Like looking in a well-lit, overly precise mirror, suddenly all I see are the open pores and the wrinkles and a tired look in the eyes. My heart sinks. I'm overwhelmed by a feeling of dread and self-loathing at the very same time that I'm supposed to be out in the world talking with great enthusiasm about my new work. After the initial post-publication depression, whether the book is heralded or skewered, sells well, or is a flop, I invariably manage to crawl out of my abyss toward the next project in an attempt to reach for something closer to the truth, better crafted, less pockmarked with imperfections.

If one day I ever do finish something that I'm 95 percent or 99 percent satisfied with, I might just throw in the towel and retire to Belize. That would surely kill me. Thankfully, I am still unsettled and happily dissatisfied.

Don't get me wrong; I am capable of learning from my mistakes. After once dropping my keys down an elevator shaft, I am more mindful of my grasp. After my first marriage ended in divorce, I understand more about what it takes to sustain and nurture a marriage. After having two Toyotas stolen in front of my house, I only buy Subarus. I've never designed a stage set that collapsed since that first time, had a book printed again grain wrong, started another meeting of two-hundred people by insulting half of them, or let the pipes freeze and burst like I did twenty-five years ago. And I'll never again vote for Ralph Nader, not even in a safe state.

As I write this meditation on failure, the ill-fated invasion and occupation of Iraq by my country has devolved into a full-fledged civil war that threatens to disable the entire Middle East and beyond. Nearly three years after the president-select declared the mission accomplished, his pre-emptive war against phantom weapons of mass destruction and terrorism continues to spread nothing but mass destruction and terror. On another potentially catastrophic front, just yesterday, scientists from the U.N. Convention on Climate Change presented their conclusive findings that global warming is unequivocal and accelerating, and surprise surprise—mankind is largely to blame. "There is no more debate about that," they said.

We don't need a crystal ball to see that we're at a crossroad of our own creation. As a species, we can continue to annihilate one another and come up with more and more lethal ways of doing so in the name of peace, god, democracy, and freedom. We can keep on cutting down our planet's trees to spite its air, poison its oceans, suck all the oil out of its core, and disrupt the very atmosphere needed to sustain us. Or, we can learn from our mistakes and make the necessary changes we already know how to make. In a way, we have come full circle back to our reptilian origins. Esoteric, sublime, even pedestrian questions about poetry, art, aesthetics, friendship, and love are threatened by a more fundamental question: Will the large human brain ultimately prove itself to be an un-survivable mutation, or will we adapt our behavior in time to save ourselves from the blowback of our own failed successes?

No Time
Failure

By David Jury

for

The last ten years in U.K. education have seen the best (and, admittedly, probably the most expensive) system of design education in the world decimated by three key factors: the introduction of free market principles, severe financial cuts, and the mismanagement of digital technology.

The pre-digital, hand-making process certainly provided ample opportunity for failure, encouraging a constant re-appraisal and re-checking before making a mark, cut, or fold. Even the act of putting everything away and spreading the various elements across a table again the next day created the opportunity to re-evaluate and discover alternative possibilities. The "sophistication" of digital technology lies in its gorgeous physical presence, super-efficient storage, and the allure of light-emitting screen. Sophistication is also suggested by the lack of physical movement it demands of its user; this sedentary working posture gives the impression that the computer is doing all the "work"—all that cutting and pasting—thus, apparently, negating the necessity of craft skills, enabling all and sundry, regardless of skill or knowledge, to produce something that appears "designed," regardless. The possibility of failure, that once constant, familiar companion of the professional designer, and so effective in keeping the mind, hand, and eye alert to every possibility, must now be consciously pursued. The homogenized outcome, torpid, commonplace, dull, is the result of bored and stressed graphic designers with no time to court failure. Creativity requires risk. Risk requires time to fail.

Unfortunately, in an attempt to make design courses more efficient, specialist studio facilities (graphics, fashion, product, etc.) and workshops such as photography and printmaking came under serious threat. The argument being that the implementation of "industry standard" digital technology could provide students with everything they needed to learn about design, but in a fraction of the time and space required by so-called traditional teaching methods. As a result, many colleges, in an attempt to appear cutting edge, eagerly cut these human- and equipment-intensive activities out of the curriculum. Measuring, drawing, cutting, creasing, folding, tearing, gluing, stitching, binding, mixing, printing ... It is astonishing that these basic coordinative skills, and the understanding they bring to the basic materials we must all use, were so close to being entirely wiped from the experience of learning to design. How could such a ludicrous situation have come about?

For those educated before the digital revolution, the college studio ethos was one of entertainment, excitement, experiment, and argument. It was where everything happened. Designing was a very public activity, and so there was plenty of opportunity for everyone to see what everyone else was doing. Such a transparent working environment ensured students built up their confidence. The development of an unconventional idea or a risky procedure created questions, criticism, and arguments.

To enable these communication skills to develop, each student had his or her own work space and access to specialist workshops on a "drop-in" basis. In this way, college was more conducive to the intellectual and practical requirements of designing than anywhere else, and so the college studio became a genuine second "home," a place where it felt quite natural to spend every weekday as well as most evenings. And do so willingly.

The digital revolution evolved at the same time that art and design education began to be radically cut back. Was this coincidence or opportunism? Any designer aged over thirty-five will be astonished to hear that full-time design education today in the U.K. requires just twelve to fourteen hours of tutor contact time per week, of which, perhaps, just six hours (one day) will usually be spent in the studio. Many colleges have lost specialist studio space altogether and ask their students to attend tutorial sessions once a week. The act of designing takes place somewhere else and quite alone.

If you are wondering how this could have happened without protest, then you must remember that whilst this was going on, the nature of higher education itself in the U.K. was dramatically changing. It had been turned into a free market. Colleges and universities found themselves in a situation where they had to recruit ever-increasing numbers of students—so many, in fact, that today every student seeking a place in a degree course in art and design will surely find one. Yes, regardless of ability! A political ideal that, I am sure, can be made to appear entirely positive on paper but that is wrecking Britain's once fine reputation for design education.

The reason no one complains is because no one is willing to suggest, not for one second, that their degree course is one of those caught up in the spiral of increasing numbers of students whilst cutting back on tutor contact time. The fear is that such public criticism of the system will adversely affect their ability to hit their recruitment targets. Instead, we all fudge and fidget.

The real world—the one where real things are made, held, and used—needs to be brought back into the studio through projects that require a knowledge of materials and the element of risk in hand-made skills to make such materials into a fully functioning object. For the graphic designer, real objects are still predominantly made from a plethora of papers available with a multitude of finishes, textures, colors, and weights and a myriad of specialist printing techniques, inks, and finishes. The printing press may be driven by digital technology, but, just like the designer's software, it is capable of infinite subtlety—if the designer only has the time to explore, and there is no better place to discover the infinite possibilities of photography and print than in the college photographic darkrooms and printmaking workshops. If the student is lucky, there will also be wood, metal, and plastics, as well as ceramics and glass workshops.

Craft areas within studios—areas that demonstrate the importance of making "things" that can, in turn, demonstrate an object's value and its effectiveness for purpose are, thank goodness, making a come-back. Unfortunately, this is too late for some colleges. The notion that the computer could do it all was always the naive dream of the opportunist college administrator who hoped to replace, for example, photographic studios, darkrooms, and specialist lecturers with a ten-pack of Photoshop. Next in line was the printmaking workshop, and any other "workshop" where students, as part of the learning experience, tested their dexterity and ingenuity beyond their abilities and got their hands dirty in the process. To the administrator, such inefficient use of time, space, and equipment was surely down to bad teaching technique, poor planning, and the neglect of health and safety regulations.

Instead, the salvation of the studio ethos will, and is, thank goodness, being achieved by giving those craft areas, which were once considered to be merely "supporting," a more central function. The computer is no longer the "magic" box, but rather the workhorse it was always intended to be. What brings students back into college, even outside taught hours, are the craft workshops that offer a learning experience that cannot be achieved anywhere else.

There is a new desire to structure timetables, modules, and projects so that emphasis is placed upon creative endeavor that is gained through an understanding of materials rather than a total reliance upon digital technology. This is achieved through a sharing of creative and technically risky procedures that the student understands are essential in avoiding the torpid, commonplace, and dull. It is essential that the student recognizes that these activities are being driven from the graphic design studio. But if implemented, the result will be higher levels of commitment, more peer involvement, and results with which the student can feel a more intimate statement of intent.

The Evolution of Useful Things: Success through Failure

By Henry Petroski

Desire, not necessity, is the mother of invention. Things and the ideas for things come from our dissatisfaction with preexisting things and from the want of a satisfactory existing thing for doing what we want done. More precisely, the development of new artifacts and new technologies follows from the failure of prior ones to perform as promised or as well as can be hoped for or imagined. Frustration and disappointment associated with the use of a tool or the performance of a system put a challenge on the table: Improve the thing. Sometimes, as when a part breaks in two, the focal point for the improvement is obvious. Other times, such as when a complex system runs disappointingly slowly, the way to speed it up may be far from clear. In all cases, however, the beginnings of a solution lie in isolating the cause of the failure and in focusing on how to avoid, obviate, remove, or circumvent it. Inventors, engineers, designers, and common users take up such problems all the time.

The earliest useful things were, of course, those found in nature. Not surprisingly, these same things became the earliest tools. Thus, rocks came to be used as hammers. Whether a particular rock makes a good hammer depends on its size and shape and on its hardness and toughness relative to the object being hammered in the task at hand. Rock types that failed to accomplish desired ends became known as poor hammers and so came to be passed over. Better hammers resulted from eliminating the failures. However, even the best of rocks have limitations as hammers, and the recognition of their failure in this regard defined the design problem: Devise a better hammer. Among the problems with a hammer-rock could be that it is awkward or uncomfortable to wield. An improvement might be sought in the shape of the rock or in providing a handle for it—or from replacing the rock with something better. In time, a growing variety of metal hammerheads and wooden hammer handles, appropriate for a variety of tasks and grips, would reflect increasing specialization and diversification. Among such diversity, one might expect that there would be a single best hammer for a particular task. All the others would fail to work as well at that task. Should all existing hammers fail to work properly for a newly developed task, then a still newer hammer might have to be developed. By the latter part of the nineteenth century, some five hundred different types of hammers were being produced in Birmingham, England, alone.

Technological systems also have their roots in the given world. The circadian and seasonal rhythms of nature drove the development of patterns of rest and migration. Even the simple act of sleeping when it is dark could be fraught with danger, however, as may have been discovered the hard way. If all the members of a group slept simultaneously, some might fail to survive the night. Recognizing this failure of the system would naturally lead to such concepts as the staggered watch and other means of protection. Thus, the group might begin sleeping in a cave whose single entrance could be guarded by a boulder rolled across it. The inconveniences of migration ultimately led to the development of systems of agriculture and defense. No matter how well developed a thing or system becomes, however, it will never be without limitations. There are no mechanical utopias. Therefore, there will always be room for improvement. The most successful improvements ultimately are those that focus on the limitations—on the failures.

Success and failure in design are intertwined. Although a focus on failure can lead to success, too great a reliance on successful precedents can lead to failure. Success is not simply the absence of failure; it also masks potential modes of failure. Emulating success may be efficacious in the short term, but such behavior invariably and surprisingly leads to failure itself. Thus, a single type of rock that worked reasonably well as a hammer for every previously known task might be said to be the hammer-rock. Whenever anyone wanted an all-purpose hammer, they would look for that type of rock, if they had not already become accustomed to carrying it around with them. In time, however, there would arise a task in which the hammer-rock would fail. This would occur, for example, when the implement was used to strike a newly discovered but harder and tougher rock, with the purpose of shattering it. But to everyone's surprise, it would be the hammer-rock itself that would shatter. Past successes, no matter how numerous and universal, are no guarantee of future performance in a new context.

Failure and responses to it may not explain every aspect of every design, but from the engineering perspective, it is a unifying theme for describing the functional evolution of things. In particular, the interplay between failure and success in the development of technological artifacts and systems is an important driving force in the inventive process. While the focus here has been on the functional, there are numerous other factors that affect design—including the aesthetic, cultural, economic, egotistical, ethical, historical, political, and psychological—but no brief essay can hope to say everything about everything.

Design a Slow-Motio Train Wrec

By Ross Macdonald

I work with type—the actual cast-in-metal-or-carved-from-wood kind of type. My design process involves taking a quick sketch or mental picture down to my pressroom, pulling open drawers and cases, setting type in a composition stick, moving things around on the bed of the press, and pulling proof after proof. After awhile, if I'm lucky, I start to get somewhere—usually after I've thrown out the sketch, the mental picture, and several rounds of type.

In the many years that I've been involved, one way or another, in letterpress, I've had many conversations with designers about working with wood and metal type. Some of them start to take on a hallowed, reverential tone. Often one of us (not me) will get a far-away look in his eyes, and words like "wonderful" and "craft" and "art" and "beauty" start coming up.

I try not to give in to the urge to snort a sardonic laugh. At this point in the conversation, I, like most letterpress people I know, will quickly trot out my excess equipment and ugly broken down type and try to make a quick sale before the mood fades—we all recognize the signs of someone who is teetering on the edge and who only needs a nudge to fall deeply into the dream of letterpress.

It's not every day you get a chance to unload all those cases of Park Avenue and Ultra Bodoni!

I, and many other letterpress people I know, have also happily cleared the dusty type and rusty presses out of the basements of many designers and others who have flirted with letterpress only to come to the slow realization that it ain't what it's cracked up to be. Usually this person is upstairs, slumped in a rocking chair, staring out the kitchen window with a glassy–eyed expression, while a couple of sweaty, dirty, true believers haul the offending lead out of the bowels of their house.

I don't mean to say that letterpress isn't art, or craft, or beauty—but those things can often come at the cost of many hours of almost soul-crushing disappointment and maddening frustration. Every successful letterpress piece I manage to pull off—every card or broadside or poster or letterhead or jam label—is almost always the end result of a few compromises, dead ends, and workarounds. It's rare that my "vision" of a beautiful piece isn't ground under the heels of the many little failures along the way.

For instance, often the "perfect" font is too big, or small, or won't fit in the measure, or is a font that you have been looking for, unsuccessfully, for years. On a computer, a couple of key strokes will take care of most problems like that. There aren't many designers these days who have to try to figure out ways to deal with the fact that the font they want to use doesn't have enough es (that's where the expression "out of sorts" actually originated) or that a mouse just had babies in the M quad compartment. Also, some older early nineteenth century display fonts were designed without figures—sometimes without punctuation. Lots of older type has been used so much (or pounded half to death, as I like to say) that

CRUSH YOUR ENEMIES WITH WOOD TYPE!

CRUSH YOUR ENEMIES
VOODOO TYPE

CRUSH YOUR ENEMIES WOOD TYPE

CRUSH YOUR ENEMIES WOOD TYPE

a lot of the characters are worn, or broken, or gone, or crushed so that they are no longer type height and won't print. Of course, there's no way of telling any of these things without actually setting the type first.

When I work on a piece, designing on the bed of the press as I go, a pile of failed attempts builds up on the stone—lines of type that wouldn't work, for one reason or another. I've learned to leave them there until after I'm done because I can make so many attempts that I'll sometimes forget what fonts I've already tried and thus reset the same line over and over in the same damn font. Maybe one part of my brain is hoping that maybe this time it'll fit! Those who don't learn from their failures are doomed to reset them.

The letterpress person who hasn't found himself bent over a comp stick at 3 AM, with tears streaming down his face, just isn't trying hard enough.

I think that's one of the reasons why so many letterpress people have fallen for the false god of computer-generated photopolymer type—and although it saddens me, I can't really blame them. It takes a certain kind and depth of mania to put up with "real" type.

However, having to work around the many failures has led to places I wouldn't otherwise have found. It forces you to try things and think in ways that you wouldn't have to if you could use any font you wanted in any size. The limits and frustrations and problems of trying to make the type work has sometimes led to beautiful elegant solutions that I would never have found on my own, and I have rarely ended up with a piece that I didn't like more than my original concept.

CRUSH YOUR ENEMIES WITH WOOD TYPE

CRUSH YOUR ENEMIES WITH WOOD TYPE!

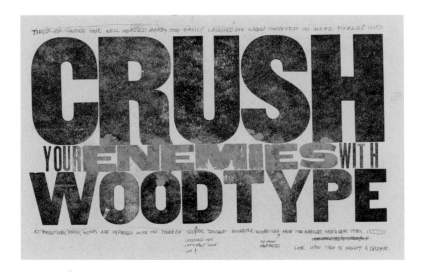

CRUSH YOUR ENEMIES WITH WOODTYPE

CRUSH YOUR ENEMIES WITH WOODTYPE!

The photopolymer crowd tends to write off us type fanatics as Luddites. They have found the clean, easy way out while the rest of us sweat and swear over the wood and lead and iron, going blind from fiddling with six-point thin spaces, our lead stained fingers digging down into the crannies of old type cases, scrabbling through the dusty mouse turds to fish out the last comma, our breath smelling of type wash fumes and that spicy wood mold that infects ancient type cabinets, and our feet numb from long hours of standing on cold concrete basement and garage floors, only to run out of lower case at three words from the end of the paragraph … and loving every minute of it.

The Nadir of My Zenith: How Great Design Failures Hath Murdered Sleep

By Francis Levy

No tube of toothpaste has ever brought me pleasure. There are everyday objects for which form transcends function, but regrettably no toothpaste—from the standup bottles that stare at you as if to proclaim I am doing my job, why do you keep asking for more? to the dented old-fashioned tubes that beach themselves on the periphery of your sink—has managed to embody anything more than a failure of design. I don't know if I can seriously discuss true design failures like MOMA or the Guggenheim. I hate Gaudi and Barcelona in general, with special emphasis on its famous shopping mall, the Ramblas. However, rather than attacking a Leviathan, let me approach those failures of imagination that just make life a little bit more miserable, like the return envelope of the Time Warner cable monthly bill and the 23rd Street Station of the IRT, which fails in its mission of bleakness.

The caduceus is one of the great failures of design (seeing snakes intertwined doesn't make me want to walk into a doctor's office), along with the crucifix, whose horrifying simplicity is not the appropriate response to something as profound as a crucifixion. By the way, isn't there any better place for a mezuzah than a doorjamb? What were mezuzah designers thinking of when they came up with a narrow object, whose embossed lettering is barely decipherable? I know there's a canon of liturgy to support most banality, but must we acquiesce—even for the sake of belief? Among the most famous failures of design in antiquity are, naturally, the Shroud of Turin and the Golden Calf. I know provenance is the point when it comes to these objects, but if you are going to demonstrate that Christ has worn something, you have to communicate, man! For instance, during the highly spiritual times of the early disco era when my philosophical outlook was shaped by a movie called Superfly, I had black zip-up boots with high heels that went along with a leather trench coat. Today we have Kim Jong Il's leisure suits, which have had an enormous impact on our perception of North Korea. That's intelligent design.

Then there was the dirty magazine section in the old Tower Books on Lafayette, which probably represents the greatest failure of quotidian design in human history. This area, located at a sharp turn in the middle of a highly trafficked section of the store, obscured the view of the bounty, thus providing camouflage for freeloaders; the resulting legacy of curled magazine corners contributed to the demise of this valuable retail outlet. And what about the flat screen TV, which murdered the last vestige of coziness epitomized

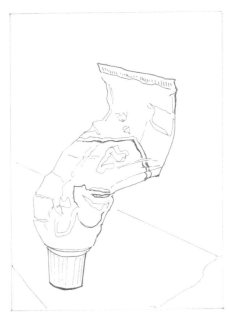

EXHIBIT A

FAILURE

EXHIBIT B

Drawings: Hallie Cohen.

153

by the small screen Zeniths of the fifties in the same way that CDs and cassettes ruined the majesty of records, as LP's clobbered 45s and 78s? Add to the list of horrors affecting the modern consumer: all pens, from Bics to expensive Parker fountains, which suffer from anonymity; bowling balls, which are sources of little more than anxiety; and escalators, which would have been a remarkable advance if they weren't limited to going up and down. One of the most notable failures of modern transportation design is the escalator in the Union Square Barnes & Noble, which at one point didn't work for months, causing a knowledge outage from lower Broadway to 23rd Street, especially with regard to the Russian literature section on the fourth floor, which was only available to the most intrepid of customers.

The stagnation of sidewalks is a source of fear and loathing that is right up there with the Swingline stapler when it comes to the category of objects that haunt to homicidal degrees. Would Meursault have exhibited one iota of discretion in *The Stranger* if he weren't so plagued by the unforgivingness of the world in which he had to walk? I have nothing against the fellow who operates the newsstand on 23rd and Sixth, with its little refrigerator full of Snapples (admittedly a drink that was a design advance if design is considered to encompass taste), but I don't know if I can endure another winter facing the indignity of standing in the cold and trying to fish into my pocket for the extra quarter while herds of the crosstown buses I'm waiting for pass me by. Failures of imagination are a little like the narrowcasting of analytic philosophy. To Wittgenstein's "What we cannot speak about we must pass over in silence," I say, "Try!"

Design is about living, and when objects fail to contribute to happiness, when loose-leafs are only as good as the paper inside them, when balls are created just to bounce (unlike the old pink Spaldings, which had great metaphysical significance to baby boomers, for whom their smell is like the Madeleine), then possession, the Rockefeller laws notwithstanding, truly becomes nine-tenths of the law and a sentence in itself.

I finish with one of the greatest design failures of my Jewish heritage: the dreydl. Dreydl, dreydl, dreydl, I made you out of clay. The dreydl illustrates the Marxian concept of man's alienation from labor. The song belies reality and has always created a misery in my spirit. I can't make a dreydl—I can barely spin one. The unwieldy physics of the object makes it impossible for a child to construct a working dreydl out of clay or anything else. Dreydls are manufactured in enormous factories by underpaid workers who care little about children and in all probability know nothing about Chanukah. The disappointment they spawn has only been palliated by the invention of another object, the milk chocolate coin, or gelt, which is bad for a child's teeth. Who ever said bad design was a victimless crime?

The Art o
the Deadl

By Alissa Walker

e

As my parents may have mentioned, I was quite an accomplished artist by the age of five. But once I succumbed to the daily regimen of kindergarten, the pressure nearly ruined my fledgling career. The joy of creating, once infinite with possibility, now came with a strict time limit.

The other kids would dutifully arrange their torn fluffs of black paper into the prescribed facial expressions of a jack o'lantern, following the three-step directions, simpletons as they were. But my plans were bigger; my proposed pumpkin, 3D. By the end of class, while the other five year olds dropped confetti trails en route to the trashcan and wondrously peeled Elmer's Glue from their fingers, I was feverishly stuffing a crinkly orange cavity full of construction paper. See, my pumpkin will really be round, I pointed to Mrs. Gold as she passed my desk. That's great, she said, but it's time to clean up. Artistic aspirations meant nothing when scheduled right before recess.

Eventually, you could take your work home with you, presenting your parents with a commissioned symbol of your love to be exhibited on the fridge gallery. But I only saw this as an extension. I'd hoard my piece-in-progress, dashing through the kitchen on my way up to my room and the auxiliary set of art supplies, while my mother tried to extract my coat. "Noooo! It's not finished, Mom!"

It was never finished.

In November, we were given thirty minutes to deliver a Thanksgiving kindergarten classic. Trace your hand here, attach beak, snood, and feathers as such, scrawl feet like upside-down pitchforks. I could hardly conceal my distain for such a tawdry representation. I shuffled the brown paper around on the page, trying to subvert the assignment. What if I created a pilgrim turkey instead? I set to work creating an anthropomorphically correct bird. But it was ambitious, even for me, and before I could even consider the graphic implications of a head, let alone a black buckled hat, we were headed to lunch. I would have to finish later.

The next morning I walked into my classroom, now draped with gourds and speckled Indian corn in anticipation of the impending feast. Suddenly, I blanched, my heart sticking to my ribcage. On a clothesline strung above our cubbies, the turkeys were clothes pinned for display, two dozen hands waving in unison.

And then there was mine: a plucked, headless turkey breast.

Too embarrassed to ask for its removal, I was forced to endure the rest of the short week knowing the misshapen poultry was looming over my shoulder. Suspended in mid-air like a frozen cutlet, the incomplete bird taught me a lesson no art teacher could. My boundless creativity was meaningless if I couldn't get it down on paper in time.

The next year, when I was in first grade, the entire school was instructed to design posters for a contest commemorating the end-of-the-year carnival. I won first place. I remember seeing it, hanging among the mostly upperclassmen finalists, its royal blue ribbon twirling in the air conditioning. I should have been proud, I suppose. But honestly, I was just glad it was finished.

bjects
lure

The Objec
of Failure

My Worst Work

By Veronique Vienne

I did what I thought was some of my best work on hands and knees. In the late 1980s, as the founding art director of *Parenting* magazine, then located in San Francisco, I often got on all fours to see the world from the perspective of babies, toddlers, and kids. I would ask photographers to get down with me and view children twenty inches from the ground. Or come eye-to-eye with a plate of mashed potatoes. Or snuggle up with a pacifier. Or get so close to a toy that it looked like a jungle gym.

In contrast, I did my worst work while trying to stay on my toes. In 1989, I left San Francisco for New York to become art director of *Self*, a Condé Nast women's magazine devoted to health and fitness. Inspired by the revved-up editorial content of the magazine, I figured that it was time to make some personal adjustments. My new position, I assumed, would require stamina and endurance—so I decided to do my work standing up or perched on a high stool. On my first day at *Self*, I cleared the desk out of my office, only keeping a long counter top as a work surface.

Unfortunately, no amount of psyching up could have prepared me for the task ahead. Anthea Disney, the editor-in-chief who had convinced me to relocate to work with her on *Self*, was fired the day the movers showed up with piles of crates and boxes that could hardly fit into my small Manhattan flat. I remember clipping the announcement of her demise in the *New York Times* with the same scissors I was using to pry open the bulging cardboard boxes.

A new, inexperienced editor was named at *Self*. She allowed imperious Condé Nast's editorial director Alexander Liberman to take over the creative direction of the magazine. Expecting me to deliver cutting-edge layouts that captured the urgency and the excitement of the moment, Liberman became increasingly frustrated with what he called my "provincial" good taste.

To survive in this abusive environment, I intensified my workout routine, now doing calisthenics at 7 AM with a personal trainer on the floor of my empty office. By the time my staff sauntered in, I was ready to wrestle every layout to the ground with my bare hands—literally. There were no computers in the art department—not yet. Creative work still involved burning calories. In fact, under Liberman's regime, designing a magazine might as well have been a contact sport. Combining text and images was a vigorous endeavor involving recalcitrant masking tape, globs of wax, layers of colored paper, slithering acetate overlays, oversized photostats, torn pieces of color xeroxes, and serendipitous fragments of graphic flotsam found in the back of forgotten drawers.

I went through a personality change. Like a hostage who embraces the cause of her kidnappers, I found myself actually liking the inane collages I was coerced to do—even though Liberman, who felt I was still too timid, would often dismiss them callously. Late at night, thoroughly humiliated, I would crawl into the backseat of some ominous limousine and, in a daze, find my way back home.

The lowest point was the April 1990 cover that Liberman decreed should be a rip-off of the *National Enquirer*. He would not leave me alone until I cropped beyond recognition a rather dull Richard Avedon's photograph of Cindy Crawford, the über model of the time, and laid on top of it a crazy patchwork of primary color blocks. The typography, a haphazard assortment of lowercase Franklin Gothic, was strewn all over the place. To top it all, the thin elongated letters of the logo were arbitrarily spaced out, beyond readability.

Meanwhile, under the new editor, readership had been dropping steadily, and someone mercifully figured it was time to fire me. Blamed for the poor newsstand performance of the magazine, I didn't argue: I accepted my share of responsibility. As I was informed that my services were no longer required, though, I felt a sense of relief. I understood in a flash that my career as an art director was over—I had paid my dues for fifteen years as a "visual communicator"—and I was free at last to become a writer.

But now, almost two decades later, as I look back at my art directorial days, I can no longer tell what was so bad about my worst work. To be perfectly candid, when I look at those old issues of *Self* done under duress, they all seem pretty good to me. Even the most maniacal spreads stand the test of time, their dreaded exuberance looking more vital and relevant today than they did in 1989.

I figured that my so-called best work was due for a revisionist look as well. So I dislodged a bound book of early *Parenting* issues from the top of my bookcase and forced myself to flip through them. It broke my heart. Yes, it looked good—the black-and-white photography in particular was inspired—but the format seemed ill-conceived. Truth be told, I had hijacked the magazine to vent my creative frustrations.

The typographic treatment was reminiscent of a genre favored then by Neville Brody in *The Face*, with stylized letterforms condensed or stretched to the max on rudimentary computer programs. The illustrations, by the likes of David Hamilton, Julian Allen, Peter de Sève, Robert Grossman, Istvan Banyai, and Robert Crumb would not have been out of place in the *Atlantic Monthly*. The photography took its cues from *Aperture* with features by Danny Lyon, Duane Michals, Antonin Kratochvil, Art Kane, and Brigitte Lacombe, and even though it all came together, rather elegantly I must say, with a muted color palette that ignored the chromatic conventions associated with childhood, it was all wrong: It presented parenting as a highly intellectual pursuit.

There is nothing that fails like success. Pride is a funny thing: One day, you too might be shamed by your very best work yet feel strangely redeemed by your worst work.

A different version of this piece was originally published in Critique in 1999.

Deathdrome.
A Video Game
Package.

By Stefan Sagmiester

I made the mistake of accepting a job I had no interest in. The standard American packaging system for a video game at the time was a jewel case inserted into a gigantic cereal box concocted to cheerfully dupe little boys into thinking they might be buying something bigger and better than a CD in an empty box.

I myself am not a gamer and could not really tell if the product we were selling was good or bad but had a hunch that it was the latter.

My first presentation to the client was somewhat below mediocre—I made another mistake and showed several possibilities—and it went downhill from there—with enough people, money, and meetings involved, we managed to quickly pass awful and moronic to end up with the remarkably pure piece of shit you see attached (I am not sure if you can show visuals). We actually designed two of these packages; I remember a full-hour meeting where grown-up employees of a multinational corporation discussed the appropriate shreddedness of shreddy bear.

Thankfully the game's life span was rather short, and it was off the shelf and consigned to the garbage bins of software history (Peter Hall in *Made You Look*) in no time.

170

PC CD-ROM

C.O.R.T.

0:00:1

DEATH DROME™

VIACOM
NEWMEDIA™

ZIPPER
INTERACTIVE

Architectural Rendering: The Failure of Imaginatio

By William Drenttel

Last year, I received an email that "The St. Lawrence Cement Plant proposal, which so many residents in the Berkshire Mountains have followed for the last six years, is now in a crucial public comment period..." It was a call to action, of course. Come to a meeting. Give money. Write your Congressman.

St. Lawrence Cement wanted to build an enormous cement plant, powered by burning coal, tires, and medical waste, on the Hudson River, about 120 miles north of New York City. The stacks on this plant were to be 406 feet tall—and being on a hill, they would loom 600 feet above the Hudson. The plume they would emit would on many days have stretched 6.3 miles, spewing as much as twenty million pounds of pollution from the project—the result of burning 500 million pounds of coal annually. Further, the Swiss corporate parent had a terrible track record of pollution and price-fixing violations worldwide. Its cement plant in

Texas, built when George W. Bush was governor, is one of the worst polluters in America.

We live thirty-five miles away from the proposed site, in the Berkshire Mountains that cross the northwest corner of Connecticut, where under moderate wind conditions the pollution would have reached us in just under an hour.

Opposition to the plant was strong from the start. Movie stars sponsored fundraisers and lent their names, including Meryl Streep and Natalie Merchant. Local newspapers wrote endless editorials. Serious environmental and health groups weighed in, including the American Cancer Society, the Natural Resources Defense Council, and the Sierra Club. There were fears that the plant would ruin historic sites like Olana, the 19th-century home of the artist Frederic Church. Even the local antique dealers association in Hudson, New York, signaled its opposition.

When I had first heard about the project several years earlier, I had urged the opposition leaders to find a way to visualize its scale and to dramatize the scope of its pollution. There were many efforts to do this.

175

There was a balloon-flight test to demonstrate the height of the towers and its resultant "blight on the landscape." There were photo simulations and photographs of modeled plumes. There were events in which building columns illustrated the stack height. Some organizations offered promotional taglines: "Stop the unhealthy reindustrialization of the Hudson Valley," for example. There were also posters by nationally recognized designers (like Woody Pirtle of Pentagram) and by local artisans, as well as numerous billboards.

Further, there were other "Stop the Plant" movements to learn from: the 325-foot stack for the proposed power plant on the Greenpoint waterfront in New York City; cement plants on the Ohio River in Cincinnati and on the Ichetucknee River in Florida; and the "Campaign Against the New Kiln" in Padeswood, Flint-shire, U.K.

Yet, across these projects, there was no single rendering ominous enough to establish public fear; no image so compelling as to create political momentum; no symbol so memorable as to unite the opposition. Whether through artistic rendering or information design, no one made a visual case against these plants that has been wholly effective.

This is, I believe, a fundamental failure of design.

Architects have a long tradition of rendering the future, of creating images that excite the public and unify political interests. Hugh Ferriss's 1940 studies for Metropolis opened the door to the modern skyscraper. In 1922, even the losing entries for the Chicago Tribune Tower were imaginatively rendered, deeply affecting architectural history for years to come (e.g., drawings by Eliel Saarinen and Adolf Loos). More recently, the Freedom Tower was emotionally rendered by Daniel Libeskind (as well as symbolically rendered in its 1776-foot height). Not all these buildings were (or will be) built. But they all excited the public imagination, creating political energy and public discourse.

My favorite recent example is the commission won by Field Operations/Diller Scofidio + Renfro for the High Line project in Chelsea, Manhattan. In their colorful renderings, imaginary beaches on the railroad tracks near the Hudson River bring Miami to mind. This is not a project one ever expects to be built with fidelity to these drawings. But these renderings did expand the conception of what disused railroad beds might be, and in the process, they galvanized the public (as well as the politicians). The High Line will be saved, in part, precisely because of such images. (One should acknowledge, as well, the dedicated photographic work of Joel Sternfeld.)

What is not said, of course, is that architecture is a forward-moving enterprise, a place in our public dialogue where we envision new beginnings. One can only imagine the drawings that will surface in the coming months and years for the new future of New Orleans. What is lost in these future-oriented scenarios is the power of architectural rendering to imagine terror and pollution and destruction. Architecture wants to fix things, build new buildings, conceive of new environments. It has little interest in its power to render the negative—to use its tools of visualization to help us not build.

Back in the Berkshire Mountains, where I live, we're lucky. Our future now looks slightly better after New York State put a stop to the St. Lawrence Cement Plant in April 2005, saying that it would harm the people, economy, and environment of the Hudson Valley. Most people here credit New York State politics, in which George Pataki, a Republican governor, desires a strong legacy of environmental action.

Nonetheless, there are still no fantasies of a Miami on the Hudson here. The images that determined our future were weak, second-rate renderings, hardly the inspired, fantastic renderings that drive most modern urban projects. We had only photographic renderings of long plumes of pollution—cotton balls hanging from miniature wires—waxing in the wind of an amateurish model.

It's hard to believe that such renderings stopped this plant or will stop other plants in the future.

This essay originally appeared on *Design Observer* in February 2005.

An Uphil
Struggle

By David Womack

The prospect of a week-long backpacking trip in the Sierra Nevada mountains inspired me to look harder at Scott, the apparel guy at Paragon Sports, than he was probably comfortable with. The question was not whether I wanted what he had to sell—in this case a Gore-Tex fleece with neoprene cuffs and inner and outer storm flaps—but whether I could live without it. As the least fit member of our group of hikers, I knew that the only way I was going to make it up a mountain was to carry as little as possible on my back.

"If I do not buy this, Scott," I shook the garment while beads of sweat formed on his upper lip, "will I die? Will I actually freeze?" Scott swallowed. Ron, the floor manager who had tried to sell me battery-powered socks, paced back and forth between knitwear and waterproofs, ready to intervene. "Scott," I whispered, "talk to me." He cleared his throat, "Listen," he said, "I was drunk, and it was February. My girlfriend wouldn't let me in. So I spent the night on a park bench with a pizza box for a pillow and this fleece on." I nodded and dropped the fleece into my basket. Three nights later on a mountaintop, when the moon rose and the temperature dipped to freezing, I was glad as hell I had.

But the fleece was the exception, and there were countless other comforts—inflatable pillows, a wire saw with tiny diamond teeth, a lantern for reading, a campfire coffee maker, even mosquito repellent—that however useful and attractive could not be proven necessary for preserving life. I had to resist my usual raccoon-like tendencies to pick up anything shiny and, for once in my life, get serious about my things.

This was a very different kind of shopping for me, and I have to say I was enjoying it. It had a raw, life-or-death edge to it that I rarely experience, even at sales. What I was putting together, to borrow Corbusier's phrase, was a machine for living, and not just living in some milk fed suburban idyll, but living in a particularly rugged swatch of 21st century ecosystem on the brink of catastrophic collapse.

As I gathered my gear, it occurred to me that we are all embarking on a similar mission of survival. It's no longer enough that the things we carry be attractive and not un-useful. Global warming will make life hotter and harder for almost everyone. The expanding population will put more pressure on dwindling resources. The Yuan will get even stronger against the dollar, causing prices to rise at Walmart. All of this will change the way we relate to basic stuff.

"Urine?" I asked the sales rep in water filters. "I don't see why not," he replied. "It's got a ceramic core." The MSR filter is a tour de force of gear design—translucent candy-red plastic that lets you follow the liquid as it slurps through the intake hose, disappears into the smooth ceramic monolith, and comes jetting out the bottom, purer than Perrier. Yes, it is true that the main competitor, the Katydyn filter, has a better flow rate, but everything with the Katydyn happens behind the scenes, hidden inside the dull beige case—there is no theater, no awareness that this device performs a miracle, transubstantiating turgid sludge into the very essence of life. Flow rate is important, but one must still save a place for magic.

The fleece and filters were just the warm-up. First aid

challenged me on a more fundamental level. The term "essential" is much more slippery than it at first lets on. Like the Republican platform, it has the ring of moral righteousness, of manly decisiveness, when really it is an uneasy compromise between fear, on the one hand, and laziness on the other. In fact, it is impossible to know what is really essential until it's too late. Take splints, for example. I have never yet needed a splint, which consists of two elegantly contoured lengths of durable plastic that can be fastened tightly around a fractured bone. Maybe the fact that I haven't yet needed a splint is exactly why I need one now. My odds are up. Writhing in pain halfway up a mountain, I can imagine myself remembering myself back at the store holding a splint. But, standing here in the store, I can also imagine myself carrying the splints up the mountain and not breaking my leg. So, as a compromise, I get the very lightweight snake-bite kit. No one can say I'm not prepared.

While my first aid kit was admittedly eccentric—in keeping with the unpredictable nature of accidents—my wardrobe was strictly utilitarian. Early on, I made the decision to sacrifice cleanliness for efficiency. I would be dirty, but I would reach the peak. I packed two pairs of quick-washing nylon bikini brief underpants, two moisture-wicking SPF 30 T-shirts, a pair of long underwear, a stocking cap which could double as an oven-mitt, two pairs of shorts, the aforementioned fleece, two pairs of socks, a hat with a wide brim, and a lightweight raincoat. The entire bundle weighed about as much as a Big Mac.

Now, through the magic of hindsight, I can reveal that I may have been a little too zealous in my efforts to purge. At the last minute, I jettisoned my Tevas, leaving me with only the one pair of hiking boots. I believe this decision reveals important lessons about aesthetics and environmental strain. You see my Tevas feature an Aztec print pattern that drives my wife Alice to distraction and causes her to act like she's being ill. For whatever reason, she really hates the Aztecs. So she caught sight of the Tevas and commenced fake barfing. I could see her point, really. For me, the whole man-sandal genre evokes the image of software engineers with ratty ponytails riding Segways through the streets of San Jose—something I would rather not take with me into the wilderness. For this reason, I did not bring a second pair of footwear. About halfway through the first day's climb, I felt a rubbing that soon became a chafing, and by the time we stopped, I had pillowy white blisters on my heels. The second day, I had to hike in my friend's fiance's camp shoes: I wore pink Crocs with swirls. With socks on. So let that be a lesson to you aesthetes. Stick to what you know is right even when it's unattractive, for even more hideous options await the unprepared.

But, before that, at the bottom of King's Canyon, standing in the parking lot with all the day-trippers driving by in their Suburbans, the tinted windows packed high with beer coolers, I swung my pack onto my back and cinched the hip strap tight around my paunch. The pack still felt pretty heavy, but I could tell you every single thing that was in it and why. There was the mountain; here was me. And all that was between us were these things.

That hiking trip has really changed the way I think about my stuff. Since I've come back down, I've found myself in the habit of lifting things. Just picking them up and putting them down again to get a sense of how much they weigh and how much space they occupy. Nothing fancy, I'm not levering up my refrigerator, although I did notice how many condiments I have in there.

I have three different kinds of crusty mustard, one and a half ketchups, and a jar of capers just sitting there. I've been spending energy to keep this stuff cold not because I want it—except for the one ketchup—but because, through the miracles of modern technology, I have never before felt them as a burden.

I tried to give the capers to my neighbor who is French. She held the jar up almost suspiciously examining the label and shaking it a little so that the capers spun. "Are you sure you do not want them? Capers, you know; they can be very nice." I explained that I didn't really cook with capers and that they were just there, consuming resources, in my fridge. Finally, almost reluctantly, she took this burden from me, and I felt, if not free, then a little less encumbered. More prepared for what's ahead.

Spinout: Was Building a Soap Box Derby Racer My Brother's Last Best Chance at Escaping His Fate?

By Colin Berry

All his life, my brother, Kevin, was plagued with terrible luck. It began when he was a teenager, and soon became something of a family legend. This was in the early 1970's, in Longmont, Colorado—our hometown—and if the Trojan theater was giving away free *Planet of the Apes* tickets, the kid in front of him in line got the last one. If Kevin sold enough newspaper subscriptions to win a clock radio, it was broken when he opened the box. If a friend shoplifted a pack of Odd Rods bubblegum cards on the way home from school, Kevin got collared for it. It was a pattern. He weathered it well, half-joking about his luck with his shy, gap-toothed grin, but over time it took a terrible toll.

In shop class, however, Kevin seemed to step from its shadow. He was adept with tools and proved himself a skilled carpenter at an early age. I was seven years younger, and remember marveling at the first projects he brought home from junior high school: a varnished gun rack; a Newton's Cradle, with its five suspended steel balls; a sturdy set of bedroom shelves for his Revell models. Looking back, it follows that the noisy, meditative setting of the woodshop would appeal to Kevin, a place where no one was shouting at him, where no electronic parts could mysteriously fail.

In our basement, Dad had a woodshop, too, a flagstone-floored, fluorescent-lit grotto with an oversized plank workbench, barrels of wood scraps, and a pegboard hung with tools. It was here, from 1969 to 1972, that my brother built four Soap Box

Derby racers. He would start in late winter, when snow still lay on the ground outside, transforming the small stack of lumber and paper sacks of hardware into a teen-sized, gravity-propelled vehicle. Balancing the shell of the car across two sawhorses, he built each the same way: a pine plank floorboard supported several plywood bulkheads, to which he anchored Masonite sides and top. Each car ran on four red-rimmed Soap Box Derby wheels, controlled by a simple cable steering system and foot-pedal drag brake. Each was painted and lettered with Kevin's name, number, and sponsor logo (Weicker Moving and Storage). And each one got faster.

Fundamentals, however, were the only thing Kevin's cars had in common. The first two (green, orange) were simple sit-down models; the next two, painted the same bronze as Weicker's moving vans, were long, elegant lie-back cars, their rear headrest supporting my brother's head, his bright blue eyes barely visible from beneath the white regulation Derby helmet.

Leaning against the doorway, I am watching him work: The aroma of fresh sawdust mixes with hot electric motor smells of the drill and jigsaw, whiffs of Plastic Wood and the rubbery tang of new wheels. The radio segues from Jerry Reed's "Amos Moses" into Led Zeppelin's "Immigrant Song"—

We come from the land of the ice and snow.

From the midnight sun where the hot springs blow—and the gentle screek screek of Kevin's file or keyhole saw drowns out the muffled voices coming from upstairs. He is fourteen; I am seven. I idolize him, of course, and even though he ignores me, rasping an axle tree into aerodynamic shape, he probably secretly enjoys having me down here with him.

After dinner, Dad would look in on him, too, but by then

the two of them already had a tempestuous relationship. With his stoic patience, my father could never—would never—understand Kevin's propensity for frustration and impulsive anger. A frozen bolt or misdrilled hole could send him into a furious rage, sabotaging many days' work in a scary tantrum. Generally he worked alone.

Kevin's labors were part of a long tradition. Started by Chevrolet in 1934, the All-American Soap Box Derby is known as the "World's Gravity Grand Prix," and in my brother's day, it was open only to boys eleven to sixteen. Its rules were strict: Cars couldn't exceed 80 inches' length or 250 pounds, including driver; materials couldn't cost more than $40. Contestants built their own cars; parents could offer advice—Kevin could check with Dad on how to laminate the nosepiece or shim the axles (as I did, seven years later)—but the regs specifically forbade adult intervention. Each boy raced in a local competition (ours was in Boulder, on Lehigh Street hill, around July 4th), and the local winner went to Akron, Ohio, for the national championship. Akron Winners received a trophy, a $7,500 college scholarship, and a white champion's jacket which, if I shut my eyes, I could almost picture Kevin wearing.

With each year, his cars got better. The last—in 1972, when he was sixteen—was magnificent, a sleek, teardrop-shaped stiletto with meticulously trued wheels, reverse-hinged rear brake, and steering system that glided gracefully in its guides. As his early racers were amateurish and hand-spray-painted, this one was elegant and sophisticated, with steel sleeves for its cables, a carpeted floorboard, and four airbrushed coats of copper auto body paint applied inside a newspaper-lined cubicle. Most boys Kevin's age couldn't have built it.

At sixteen, Kevin was tilting towards trouble. He already had his learner's permit, and had begun associating with boys who drove real cars, and smoked Winstons, and hung out in his attic room, laughing and talking and listening to what would someday be called Classic Rock. Sometimes they would disappear for a while in Carl Kleveno's blue Duster, returning with red-rimmed eyes and smelling smoky and sweet. Though we never mentioned it aloud, my family knew the 1972 Derby marked the end of something, and convinced ourselves it was Kevin's last best chance to win.

Race day dawned dry and cloudless. After Dad and Kevin chocked his car carefully into the Fairlane and Mom and my sisters packed tuna sandwiches and a Thermos of milk into the Chevelle, we caravanned to Boulder, securing a spot near the bottom of Lehigh where we could see the finish line. The mood was playful and competitive, spectators mixing with the young racers.

In his preliminaries, my brother clocked a better time than anyone, three-fourths more than two seconds faster than the next contender, Bobby Lange, Jr., a rich kid from Boulder with a shiny fiberglass car and a cocky attitude. Kevin won his first few heats easily, a copper blur shooting past the finish line, past the checkered flag, and past his sunburned family, who waved and screamed like demons.

"Come on, Kevin!"

"Go! Go! Goooo!"

"Keviiiiiiiiin!"

And the winner is Kevin Berry, Weicker Moving and Storage!

With nearly thirty boys competing, the double-elimination race seemed to crawl. Still, I remember feeling it was marching towards Kevin's inevitable victory and, although I wasn't conscious of it, an almost tangible lifting of his tainted luck.

Sometime after 3:00 PM, after an endless succession of heats, only six cars remained: Kevin's, Lange's and four others. On one race, however, as Kevin sped past, I saw something strange happen: Just past the finish line, his car pulled suddenly to the left, and rather than braking normally, swerved and plowed into the hay bales piled at the bottom of the hill. Dad and I dropped our pops and sprinted to him.

Dad got there first. "You all right, Kev?" He sounded worried.

My brother had pulled his helmet off, his face sweaty and pale. He was clearly distressed. "I'm okay, but I think the car's messed up," he said. "I'm not sure what happened."

Race officials ran over, pulling bales off the car and lifting Kevin out carefully. He wasn't hurt, but as they rolled his car away, its rear wheels made a jarring shudder. Something was wrong.

"Look at that!" Kevin moaned, pointing, and Dad and I looked: Freshly splintered wood protruded from the foam rubber padding where the axle met the body. Somehow his brake had failed, and the crash had torqued the car badly out of alignment.

That was it. Kevin lost his next race by two car lengths, and half an hour later Bobby Lange was the 1972 Boulder champion. I remember riding home in stony silence.

The story could end there—and in a way it did, at least for Kevin. In August, he bought his first real car, a '61 Buick Special, using money he'd made working at Marcantonio's Pizza on North Main. Bobby Lange won in Akron, too; the Boulder Daily Camera printed a picture of him, smiling and waving and wearing the white jacket. Kevin's racer went up on blocks.

We didn't pay much attention at first, but the next year, 1973, Bobby Lange's cousin, Jimmy Gronen, also won the Boulder race and went on to win Akron as well. Yet officials had noticed a strange lurch as Gronen's car came off the metal starting blocks, and the next day, they X-rayed it and discovered a powerful electro-magnet hidden inside the nose of the car. It was wired to a switch Jimmy's head activated as he lay back in his headrest and gave him a jump off the line.

The scandal rocked the Derby. Gronen was stripped of his title, his winnings given to the second-place finisher. But the real blame fell on Jimmy's guardian uncle, ski-boot magnate Robert Lange, Sr.—Bobby's father. In legal documents and public state-ments, the elder Lange took full responsibility for the magnet's idea (though not its construction), pointing out with indignation that cheating was endemic to the Derby. At some point, officials asked to X-ray Bobby's 1972 car, too—the car that had beaten my brother's—which the D.A. found during his investigation had been built with $10,000 to $20,000 worth of engineering expertise. This was clearly beyond the rules. Though Derby cars are usually preserved for promotion, Bobby's car was nowhere to be found, and remains so today.

None of this really mattered to Kevin. He was past all that, enmeshed in a teenager's life filled with the cars, cigarettes, beer, and drugs mid-1970's kids suddenly had to contend with. Within two years, Kevin had accumulated a reckless driving citation, a DUI, a trip to the police station, and a long succession of real cars, some of them wrecked. Like the radio signal from an interplanetary probe that passes behind a planet, his bad luck, which had seemed to disappear for a while, was back, loud and clear.

Kevin barely graduated from high school, taking a series of jobs working for heating contractors until his patience wore thin. He didn't build much of anything after that—a shingled camper for his pick-up, a metal tool box for Dad—and didn't seem to have any hobbies. He and I grew distant. His friends seemed to disintegrate into desperation or suicide and, in 1998, he did, too, with a .22 pistol in the small, neat bedroom of his trailer on the outskirts of Boulder. He died in January, confessing in his note that he couldn't stand working outside in the cold anymore.

What would have happened to Kevin if things had unfolded differently that July day in 1972? How much would have changed? What happened to his brake? Why did it fail? And if it hadn't, could he have beaten Bobby Lange, even if—and it's all if, of course—Lange was cheating? Questions pile up like January snow, obfuscating any real truths and forcing those of us who knew Kevin to turn over a thousand times in our minds the ways it might have gone better. In a way, we—his family—are most to blame for the way we perpetuated Kevin's bad luck in our stories and expectations, allowing it to poke through even as he tried to build something solid against it. Just once, we might have speculated how that long bronze car might have carried him into something better.

Despite the scandal, the Derby has survived, though altered almost beyond recognition: Cars are built with kits now, and boys and girls from eight to seventeen compete, rally-style, in three different divisions. The rules for each comprises a massive PDF file, and kits start at $400—not including wheels, which cost up to $100 a set.

Even in Kevin's day, Soap Box Derby wheels were something singular. Every year he was issued a new set, and when the car was ready, balancing there on its planks, he would slide the new wheels onto their axles, secure the cotter pins, and give them their first long spin. They would whirl for countless minutes—half an hour sometimes, an extended low hiss like the sound of a distant crowd cheering. There in the dusty woodshop, it was a sound my brother and I hoped would last forever.

From *Make* magazine, Volume 7 (Fall 2006).

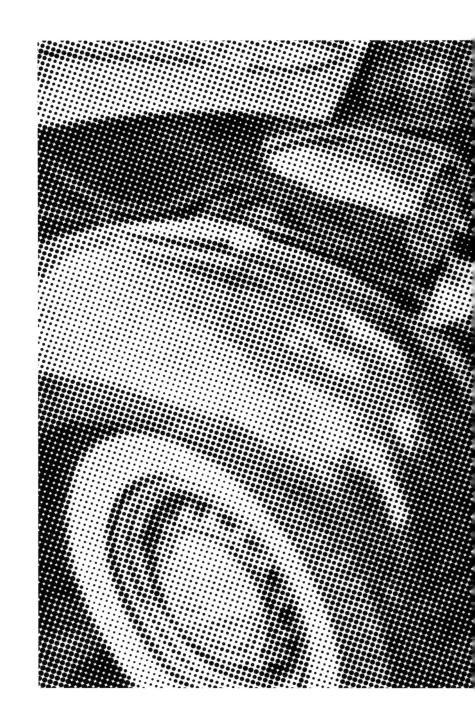

BIOGRA PHIES

Marian Bantjes has been variously described as a typographer, designer, artist and writer. Working from her base on a small island off the west coast of Canada, her personal, obsessive, and sometimes strange graphic work has brought her international recognition. Following her interests in complexity and structure, Marian is known for her custom typography, detailed and lovingly precise vector art, her obsessive hand work and her patterning and ornament.

David Barringer is the author of the novels *American Home Life* and *Johnny Red*, the book of design criticism *American Mutt Barks in the Yard*, and the fiction collections *Twisted Fun and We Were Ugly So We Made Beautiful Things*. He has written for *I.D. Magazine*, AIGA's *Voice*, *Emigre*, *Eye Magazine*, and many other periodicals. He is the senior editor and designer of *Opium Magazine* and the creator of the Dead Bug Funeral Kit. He lives in North Carolina. His Web site is *www.davidbarringer.com*.

Colin Berry is a memoirist, fiction writer, and arts journalist living in Los Angeles, California. "Spinout" is one of a series of pieces written about his family; it originally appeared in Make magazine. Colin writes for National Public Radio, *Print*, *I.D.*, *CMYK*, and *Artweek*, and is the co-author (with Isabel Samaras) of *On Tender Hooks* (Chronicle Books, 2009).

Peter Blegvad is an artist, writer, musician, broadcaster, and pedagogue. He was born in New York City in 1951. He now lives in London. His *The Book of Leviathan* was published in the United States by Overlook Press.

Ralph Caplan, upon graduating from Earlham College in 1949, was immediately asked to return to give a convocation lecture on "How to Avoid an Education." His association with failure has increased steadily ever since. A long-time chronicler of design disasters, Caplan is the author of *Cracking the Whip*, a collection of essays of design and its side effects.

Allan Chochinov is a partner at Core77, a New York-based design network supporting the global design community through both online and offline initiatives. He serves as the editor-in-chief of *Core77.com*, the widely-read design Web site, *Coroflot.com* design job and portfolio site, and *DesignDirectory.com* design firm database.

Nick Currie is a musician who has released twenty albums over the last twenty years under the name of Momus. Recently he's developed a sideline in journalism, writing for *Wired News*, *I.D.*, *Frieze*, and blogging for the *New York Times*. His own blog, *Click Opera*, was selected as a "masterwork of the Web" by Sarah Boxer. In 2009 he'll publish two books, *The Book of Jokes* and *The Book of Scotlands*.

William Drenttel is a partner in Winterhouse in Falls Village, Connecticut. He is president emeritus of the American Institute of Graphic Arts, a trustee of the Cooper-Hewitt National Design Museum, and a fellow of the Institute for the Humanities at New York University.

Ken Garland was Art Director of *Design* magazine (London) from 1956-62, when he left to establish his own graphic design studio as Ken Garland and Associates. He has contributed many articles to design periodicals in the United Kingdom, the United States, and Europe. His own publications include *First Things First* (1964), *Mr. Beck's Underground Map* (1994), *A Word in Your Eye* (1996), and *Metaphors: A Portfolio of Text and Image* (2001). He has lectured widely in the United Kingdom, the United States, and Canada, and is currently the Visiting Professor in Information Design at the Universidad de las Americas, Mexico.

Robert Grossman served a brief stint as an assistant to *New Yorker* art director James Geraghty, Grossman launched himself as a freelance illustrator and cartoonist, his work featuring caricature and a satiric outlook. Early clients included *Esquire* and the *New York Herald Tribune*. He has done cover illustrations for more than five-hundred issues of national magazines such as *Time*, *Newsweek*, *Sports Illustrated*, *Rolling Stone,* and the *New Republic*. Today his work can be seen regularly in *The Nation*, the *New York Times* and the *New York Observer*. He was nominated for a 1978 Academy Award for a brief animated film entitled *Jimmy The C*, and during the 1980's produced a number of animated television commercials. In 1979 he had a one-man show at the Vontobel Gallery in Zurich.

His sculpture and paintings in oils have been widely exhibited in numerous group shows.

Steven Heller is the co-founder and co-chair (with Lita Talarico) of the MFA Designer as Author and co-founder (with Alice Twemlow) of the MFA in Design Criticism—D-Crit—programs at the School of Visual Arts, New York. He was an art director at the New York Times for 33 years, and currently writes the "Visuals" column for the *New York Times Book Review* and is a contributor to "Campaign Stops" on the Times's online Opinion page. He is a contributing editor to *Print*, *EYE*, *I.D.*, and *Baseline* magazines and has authored or co-authored over 120 books on design and popular culture. His most recent is *Iron Fists: Branding the Twentieth Century Totalitarian State*.

David Jury is a writer, designer and educator. He is head of Graphic Media at Colchester School of Art & Design, editor of the journal *TypoGraphic,* and proprietor of the Fox Ash Press. His books include *About Face: Reviving the Rules of Typography*, *Letterpress: The Allure of the Handmade*, and *What is Typography?*, all published by Rotovision.

Benjamin Kessler is the managing editor of *Graphics.com*, a Web site for the graphic-design industry with articles, tutorials, forums, and job listings. He blogs on Graphic Design Forum. His essays on culture and politics have appeared in the newspaper *First of the Month*, among other venues. He is also a playwright whose works have been performed in New York and Los Angeles.

Warren Lehrer is a writer and designer known as a pioneer in the fields of visual literature and design authorship. His books, acclaimed for capturing the shape of thought and reuniting the traditions of storytelling with the printed page, include: *Crossing the BLVD*, *The Portrait Series*, *GRRRHHHH*, *French Fries*, *I Mean You Know*, and *Versations*. He has received many awards for his books and multimedia projects including the Brendan Gill Prize, the Innovative Use of Archives Award, a Media That Matters Award, three AIGA Book Awards, two Type Director's Club Awards, the International Book Design Award, a Prix Arts Electronica Award, and grants and fellowships from the National Endowment for the Arts, New York State Council and Foundation for the Arts, and the Rockefeller, Ford, Greenwall, and Furthermore Foundations. He is head of the design program at SUNY Purchase, a founding faculty member of the *Designer as Author* graduate program at SVA, and co-founder (with Judith Sloan) of EarSay, a non-profit arts organization dedicated to portraying the lives of the uncelebrated in print, on stage, on radio, in exhibitions, electronic media, and through educational programs in public schools, prisons, and community centers.

Francis Levy's humor, short stories, reviews, essays and poetry have appeared in the *New York Times*, the *Washington Post*, the *New Republic*, the *Village Voice*, and the *East Hampton Star*.

Ross MacDonald is an author, illustrator and designer. He has also worked as a prop maker and as a consultant on period printing, design, and documents for movies including *Seabiscuit*, *The Alamo*, *Mr. Brooks*, *Infamous*, and *National Treasure 2: Book of Secrets*. His

Illustrations have appeared in the *New Yorker*, the *New York Times*, *Rolling Stone*, *Harper's*, the *Atlantic Monthly*, and many other publications, and he is a contributing editor of the *Virginia Quarterly Review* and is on the masthead of *Vanity Fair* magazine as a contributing artist. He lives in Connecticut with his wife, two kids, dogs, cats, and a barn full of 19th century type and printing equipment.

Rick Meyerowitz was born in the Bronx, New York and studied fine arts at Boston University. Rick was the most prolific contributor of illustrated articles to the *National Lampoon* magazine. He created the poster for the movie *Animal House*, and the Lampoon's trademark visual, *The Mona Gorilla*. Rick and Maira Kalman created the most talked about *New Yorker* cover in years, "New Yorkistan." The *New York Times* wrote, "When their cover came out, a dark cloud seemed to lift." His forthcoming book, *DRUNK STONED BRILLIANT DEAD, The Writers and Artists Who Made the National Lampoon So Insanely Great* will be published by Harry N. Abrams in 2009.

Debbie Millman is the President of the Design division of Sterling Brands, the author of the book *How To Think Like A Great Graphic Designer* (Allworth Press) and the host of the Internet radio show "Design Matters." She is very motivated by her fear of failure.

Henry Petroski, the Aleksandar S. Vesic Professor of Civil Engineering and a professor of history at Duke University, is the author of *Success through Failure: The Paradox of Design* (Princeton University Press, 2006), from which this essay has been adapted. His other books on engineering and design include a technical and cultural history of the toothpick, to be published by Alfred A. Knopf in fall 2007.

Stefan Sagmeister formed the New York-based Sagmeister, Inc. in 1993 and has since designed for clients as diverse as the Rolling Stones, HBO, and the Guggenheim Museum. Having been nominated five times for the Grammys he finally won one for the Talking Heads boxed set. He also earned practically every important international design award. In the beginning of 2008 a comprehensive book titled *Things I have Learned in My Life So Far* was published by Abrams. Solo shows on Sagmeister, Inc.'s work have been mounted in Zurich, Vienna, New York, Berlin, Tokyo, Osaka, Prague, Cologne, Seoul and Miami. He teaches in the graduate department of the School of Visual Art in New York and lectures extensively on all continents.

Ina Saltz is an art director, designer, writer, photographer, and professor of Electronic Design & Multimedia (at The City College of New York) whose areas of expertise are typography and magazine design. She's a regular columnist for *STEP Inside Design* magazine and writes for other design magazines, including *Graphis*. For over twenty years she was an editorial design director at such magazines as *Time* (International Editions), *Worth*, and *Golf*, among others. She is on the design faculty at Stanford University's publishing course and also lectures for Stanford virtually via webcast. She is the author, designer, and principal photographer of *Body Type: Intimate Messages Etched in Flesh*, the first book to document typographic tattoos, published in 2006 by Harry N. Abrams Books.

Rob Trostle is a graduate student at the Yale School of Art exploring the generative aspects of failure as his thesis. He grew up in Texas and owes pretty much everything to his parents.

Véronique Vienne worked at a number of U.S. magazines as art director, including *Parenting, Self,* and the Sunday magazine of the *San Francisco Examiner.* She has written extensively on design and cultural trends. She has edited, art-directed and written essays for a number of design publications (*House&Garden, Emigré, Communication Arts, Eye, Graphis, Aperture, Metropolis, Etapes, Print, etc.*). The author of several books on design, she also writes mass-market guidebooks, including *The Art of Doing Nothing,* translated in eight languages. She lives in Paris, France.

Alissa Walker is a design writer who contributes to magazines like *Good, Fast Company, I.D.,* and *ReadyMade,* the public radio show "DnA: Design and Architecture" and her blog, Gelatobaby. She lives in Hollywood, California, where she throws ice cream socials, tends to drought-tolerant gardens, and relishes life in Los Angeles without a car.

David Womack is a writer, editor and consultant who contributes articles on design, technology, and culture to publications including *Eye, I.D.* magazine, *Salon.com, The Guardian* newspaper, and *Cabinet Magazine.* He edits *Adobe ThinkTank,* a journal that focuses on trends and developments in design and technology. David has an MFA in creative writing from the University of Virginia.

Richard Saul Wurman coined the term "Information Architect." In 1962, when he published his first book, he began the singular passion of his life: making information understandable. He chaired the International Design Conference in Aspen in 1972, the first Federal Design Assembly in 1973, followed by the National AIA Convention in 1976, before creating and chairing TED (Technology/Entertainment/Design) conferences from 1984-2002. He created and chaired the TEDMED and eg2006 conferences. He has published eighty-one books, each with a focus on understanding. He is the author of *Anxiety* and the award-winning *Access Travel Guides*. Other publications include *UNDERSTANDING USA, Urban Atlas, Wall Street Journal Access, Information Anxiety2, Diagnostic Tests for Men, Diagnostic Tests for Women, Heart Disease & Cardiovascular Health and Wills, Trusts & Estate Planning, UNDERSTANDING Children* and *UNDERSTANDING Healthcare.* He has been awarded several grants from the National Endowment for the Arts, a Guggenheim Fellowship, two Graham Fellowships, two Chandler Fellowships, and the Chrysler Design Award in 1996. In 1991, he received the Kevin Lynch Award from MIT and was honored by a retrospective exhibition of his work at the AXIS Design Gallery in Tokyo, Japan on the occasion of their 10th Anniversary. He received a Doctorate of Fine Arts by the University of the Arts in Philadelphia, an Honorary Doctorate of Letters from Art Center College of Design, and an Honorary Doctorate of Fine Arts from the Art Institute of Boston.

Index

Books from Allworth Press

Graphic Design Time Line: A Century of Design Milestones
by Steven Heller and Elinor Pettit (softcover, 6 x 9 7/8, 256 pages, $19.95)

Graphic Design and Reading: Explorations of an Uneasy Relationship
edited by Gunnar Swanson (softcover, 6 x 9 7/8, 240 pages, $19.95)

Design Connoisseur: An Eclectic Collection of Imagery and Type
by Steven Heller and Louise Fili (softcover, 7 x 9 3/8, 208 pages, $19.95)

Design Literacy (continued): Understanding Graphic Design
by Steven Heller (softcover, 6 x 9 7/8, 296 pages, $19.95)

Design Literacy: Understanding Graphic Design
by Steven Heller and Karen Pomeroy (softcover, 6 x 9 7/8, 288 pages, $19.95)

The Education of a Graphic Designer
edited by Steven Heller (softcover, 6 x 9 7/8, 288 pages, $18.95)

The Swastika: Symbol Beyond Redemption?
by Steven Heller (hardcover, 6 x 9, 176 pages, $21.95)

Sex Appeal: The Art of Allure in Graphic and Advertising Design
by Steven Heller (softcover, 6 x 9 7/8, 288 pages, $18.95)

Design Culture: An Anthology of Writing from the AIGA Journal of Graphic Design
edited by Steven Heller and Marie Finamore (softcover, 6 x 9 7/8, 320 pages, $19.95)

Looking Closer 3: Classic Writings on Graphic Design
edited by Michael Bierut, Jessica Helfand, Steven Heller, and Rick Poynor (softcover, 6 x 9 7/8, 304 pages, $18.95)

Please write to request our free catalog. To order by credit card, call 1-800-491-2808 or send a check or money order to Allworth Press, 10 East 23rd Street, Suite 510, New York, NY 10010. Include $5 for shipping and handling for the first book ordered and $1 for each additional book. Ten dollars plus $1 for each additional book if ordering from Canada. New York State residents must add sales tax. To see our complete catalog on the World Wide Web, or to order online, you can find us at *www.allworth.com*.